How a ch
Redfish

in the Indian River Lagoon System:
-The Indian River Lagoon
-The Mosquito Lagoon
-The Banana River Lagoon
A Complete Guide for the Fisherman
by John Kumiski

Argonaut Publishing Company
Chuluota, FL
www.spottedtail.com

How and Where to Catch Redfish in the Indian River Lagoon System: A Complete Guide for the Fisherman

BY JOHN A. KUMISKI

Published by: Argonaut Publishing Company
284 Clearview Road
Chuluota, FL 32766
U.S.A.

Publisher's Cataloging in Publication Data
Kumiski, John A., 1952-
How and Where to Catch Redfish in the Indian River Lagoon System
/ by John A. Kumiski.
    p. cm.
    Includes bibliographical references and index.
    Preassigned LCCN:
    ISBN 0-9635118-9-0
    1. Saltwater fishing--Florida--Guidebooks. 2.
Florida-- Guidebooks. I. Title.

WARNING! DISCLAIMER

This book is designed to provide information in regard to the subject matter covered. It is not, and was never intended to be, a substitute for good judgment or common sense. The reader ventures into or onto the water at his or her own risk.

Every effort has been made to make this book as complete and as accurate as possible. However, there may be mistakes both typographical and in content. Therefore, this book should be used only as a general guide and not as the ultimate source of boating or fishing information.

The purpose of this book is to educate and entertain. The author and Argonaut Publishing Company shall have neither liability nor responsibility to any person with any loss or damage caused, or alleged to be caused, directly or indirectly by the information contained in this book. If the reader does not wish to be bound by the above, he may return this book to Argonaut Publishing Company for a complete refund.

Table of Contents

On the cover: Rodney Smith with a fine Banana River Lagoon redfish.

Introduction

Dear Reader-

You're holding in your hand a little book that tells you everything I've learned in a lifetime of fishing, over 20 years of it in the Indian River Lagoon, about how to catch redfish. A lot of that time was spent in the "do it yourself mode", but I have had the pleasure of fishing with many, many excellent anglers through the years, many of whom are well known guides in their own right. I have learned from all of them, and I have learned from my many mistakes, and I here pass that information on to you.

I've tried to include information here to make this little book useful to everyone, from weekend truck fishermen chucking chunk bait to ritzy fly anglers in expensive skiffs heaving hackle. One of the great things about the redfish is that in the wide spectrum of angling approaches, many techniques will work. Of course some methods work better than others. But as the late Harry Truman said, "All men are created equal in the eyes of the fish," and the redfish is a democratic sort if ever there was one.

So while this book contains what 20 plus years of Florida fishing has taught me about how to catch redfish, hopefully it will tell you everything you need to know to catch more redfish, more often, and have more fun doing it. Best of luck to you!

While you're out on the water please remember the law, etiquette, and sportsmanship. Treat others like you would like to be treated. Clean up not only your mess but the one that you found when you got there. Take a child fishing. And just because you caught it doesn't mean you have to kill it. When practiced carefully catch and release works and is a wonderful way to insure that there will be some fish left in the Indian River Lagoon system next year, and the year after, and the year after that, and on and on. Fishing is usually more fun when you get bites!

Thanks for reading, and enjoy!

John Kumiski
September, 2005

Acknowledgements

This book was basically an independent project.

But thanks need to go to all the other fishermen who have taught me about catching redfish in the 20 plus years that I've been lucky enough to live in central Florida, fishermen from all over the southeastern United States, from Louisiana to North Carolina. They have all taught me a lot. And of course thanks need to go to all those fishermen who have hired me as a guide during that time, trusting me with their valuable fishing time. I hope that at least some of you found the expense worthwhile.

Finally, thanks go to my wife, Susan, for understanding the crazy lifestyle, schedule, and cash flow of a fishing guide/writer, and to my sons Maxx and Alex. Not only are they great fishing buddies and photography models, they keep me focused on the fact that in the big picture family is more important than fishing or almost anything else.

Part One: The Hardware

Spin, Plug, or Fly?

Technically speaking, you don't even need a rod or a reel in order to fish. During my travels in South America, and in south Florida for that matter, I saw many people using handlines, usually using a spark plug for a casting weight, with a can or a bottle to wrap the heavy line on. Cane poles are still popular throughout much of Florida.

Most of us get more pleasure from our fishing by using a rod and reel though. In central Florida spinning tackle is the most popular and easiest to use. Plugging (bait casting, to you old timers) tackle requires more skill and is less popular, and fly tackle requires the most skill and is least popular. They all work.

The fish don't care what kind of tackle you use. If you can use your tackle to get a bait, either real or artificial, out in front of a fish or a group of fish in such a manner that they are fooled into striking it, if you are comfortable using it, then that's what you should use.

Truck fishermen seem to prefer heavier tackle than I would recommend for redfishing of any kind. Of course, truck fishermen don't cast very often, nor do they hold the weight of the rod and reel very much. They cast their bait out, then put the rod in a holder and wait for a bite. Truck fishermen seem more concerned with putting meat on the table than with the finer points of angling, and a heavier rod and line make those fillets more of a certainty after a hookup.

Waders and anglers fishing from boats are usually holding the rod and reel combo and casting more or less continuously, so the weight or lack of weight of the outfit becomes important. For most redfishing in the Indian River Lagoon (IRL from here on out) system, I would recommend the following in the way of tackle:

Type of Tackle	Rods	Reels
Spin	6 1/2-7 1/2 feet for 10-14 lb. line	Quality reel holding +/-200 yards of mono, ex. Stradic 3000 or 4000
Plug	6-7 feet for 12-20 lb. line	Quality reel holding +/-150 yards of mono, ex. Calcutta 251 or 400
Fly	9 foot for a 7 or 8 weight line	Quality reel holding fly line and at least 100 yds 20 lb backing

Spin, plug, or fly tackle, they all work when used correctly.

Hopefully it was noticed in every case I said quality. The difference between junk and quality isn't always noticed right away. Sometimes you have to use the product for a while before any flaws appear. You can be sure that if you use a reel or rod in the IRL that isn't good quality, the salt from the water will quickly work its magic on the item. Then that item will no longer function properly.

Line

You also noticed that in the line section monofilament was listed. I imagine that monofilament is still the standard, and of course it still works. But the braided lines (Power Pro, for example) are so superior to monofilament in their performance characteristics that I never use monofilament on my spinning reels any more. If you choose to use these lines you will have to learn some new knots, and you will have to be able to untangle the bird's nests that you will occasionally get, but I find these small prices to pay for the longevity, lack of line twist, lack of stretch, and superior strength and sensitivity that these lines offer. If you are past the novice stage of angling you ought to give the braided lines an honest try.

If you use monofilament spend the extra money to buy a premium line. You can save a little bit of money by buying quarter pound spools. Keep the spool in a beer coolie (those foam covers that keep beer cans cold) and it will last a long time.

Change monofilament frequently– after every big fish, or after a month's (or two) use. Big fish trash the line, stretching it past its recovery point, twisting it (with spinning tackle at least), and heating and abrading it against the rod guides. The ultraviolet rays from the sun break down the chemical bonds within the line that hold it together.

When you consider all the expenses associated with fishing, monofilament is very inexpensive. Don't try to cut corners there, or a good fish will make you pay.

You'll get maximum casting distance by keeping your reel spool as full as possible, regardless of what kind of line you use. A full spool causes less friction, and less friction means more distance. You'll also get maximum distance by using the thinnest line possible. Thin lines break more easily than do thicker ones, so how you deal with the compromise needed here is entirely up to you. To express it simply:

Thick lines= less casting distance=less breakage.

Thin lines=more casting distance=more breakage.

Your choice.

The braided lines have more strength for a given diameter when compared to mono lines. You can use a thinner line and not lose anything in the strength department. This results in better casting distance.

Regardless of what kind of line you use you're probably going to need a leader. So let's take a look at this important piece of tackle.

Leaders

Redfish have teeth, but they don't have sharp or cutting teeth the way bluefish, mackerel, or sharks do. So a bite leader isn't needed for them. Depending on where in the IRL you're fishing you may run into other fish that do require a bite leader, but for reds you'd never need a heavier leader than 20 pound test. Where the water is very clear (during the winter for example) a thinner leader is better. Twelve pound is not too light if the fish are being tight lipped.

Fluorocarbon is recommended for leader use. It's more abrasion resistant than monofilament, so you'll land more fish. The fish cannot see it as well, based on my own tests and experience, so you'll get more bites.

Why use a leader at all? If you use a braided (or fly) line it offers a nearly invisible connection between the line and the bait. If you use monofilament it's not quite as important. However, if you use 10 pound test line with a 15 pound test leader, you'll have more strength and more margin for error at the place on the line where most of the wear and tear occurs. It's an inexpensive insurance policy for you.

Use a knot to connect the line to the leader. Hardware (such as a swivel) is prone to failure, is inelegant, and will cost you fish. If you don't have a good reason to use a swivel, don't. If you don't know what knot to use, consult a knot book.*

How long should the leader be? For conventional tackle I like mine to be most of the length of the rod when I first tie it on. As long as it will cast through the guides well it's fine. As you change hooks and lures it gets shorter and shorter until it needs replacement.

* Stren and Ande both have free knot books available, and Stren also has knot instructions on their web site, www.stren.com. An excellent book you can purchase which has every knot you could ever conceivably need is Practical Fishing Knots by Mark Sosin and Lefty Kreh.

Fishing with Bait

We can assume with reasonable certainty that the more of a fish's senses you appeal to the more likely it is that the fish will take what you're offering. A live fish, shrimp, or crab in the proper size range appeals to a redfish's senses of sight (he can see it), smell (he smells the blood or juice from the bait), and feel (his lateral line picks up vibrations from the moving bait). If the redfish takes the bait into its mouth then taste gets added to the mix. Bait is food, and it's effective for that reason.

Bait need not be alive to work though. Dead shrimp, even frozen dead shrimp, are frequently just as effective as live ones. Dead crabs, even frozen dead crabs, even pieces of frozen dead crabs, are very often effective. Chunks of bait fish, even if they have been frozen, work extremely well as redfish bait.

My anglers question me about dead bait use sometimes. My standard response is, "Think of it in terms of yourself. Do you want to catch and kill the cow, or do you want it served hot and sizzling on a platter?" They immediately get my drift.

A redfish need do nothing more than open his mouth and inhale in order to take a dead bait. Most of the time they don't mind doing this. If you use a live mullet, especially if it's livelined, the fish has to chase it down and catch it. Frankly, much of the time they can't be bothered. I rarely find mullet in the stomachs of redfish I clean, and I check every single one I kill.

Since dead bait is effective, it's very convenient for the fisherman. Anytime you get bait and then don't use it, you simply drop it into a ziplock bag and put it into the freezer (check with the wife first, obviously) for future reference. When the mullet run in the fall you can easily catch enough bait for several fishing trips, enough to get you through the winter months when mullet and other bait fish are scarce.

I stated above that I check the stomach contents of every redfish I kill. I've done this for years, and while I haven't kept a log or anything like that, my generalized observations are as follows. About 25 percent of the time the fish are empty, with absolutely nothing in the stomach or intestines. When they have food in them, it's roughly 30 percent small fish, 30 percent shrimp, and 30 percent crabs.

Generally the fish are more prevalent during the summer and fall, and the shrimp are more common in the winter and spring. Crabs, all kinds, including swimming crabs like the blue crabs and their relatives, mud crabs, small horseshoe crabs, spider crabs, and others are evidently eaten whenever they're encountered.

The other 10 percent was left for oddities. I've found various types of marine worms in redfish stomachs. I cleaned one that had two sea horses in it. I cleaned one that had eaten a large giant water bug. One had a small American eel one time. I've cleaned several that had legs of large horseshoe crabs in them. If it looks like food and they're hungry they'll eat it.

Keep in mind that all the fish that I've looked inside have been legal, in-the-slot fish between 18 and 27 inches long, two to three years old. If you were to check in the stomachs of five inch fish, or 40 inch fish, the situation might be different.

Types of Bait

For the purposes of our discussion we're looking at three main classes of bait– shrimp, crabs, and bait fish. Let's take a look at the different types of bait, how to obtain them, and how to use them.

-Shrimp. The easiest way to get this popular bait is to pick up one or several dozen at the bait shop. Redfish definitely like to eat shrimp. So does every other type of fish in the lagoon system, including such popular species as sting rays, toadfish, catfish, pinfish, and puffers. These unwanted species will rob you blind, especially during the summer months.

I find shrimp most useful for sight-fishing: that is, casting them into the path of fish that you can see. They are also widely used with a popping cork. You can also use them with a sliding egg sinker rig, but you'll get pecked to death by pinfish, blowfish, catfish, sting rays, etc.

One good thing about using live shrimp for bait is that the ones you have left over can be taken home and eaten. This is something you probably wouldn't want to do with menhaden or worms.

Two popular ways to hook live shrimp that you want to stay that way are as follows:

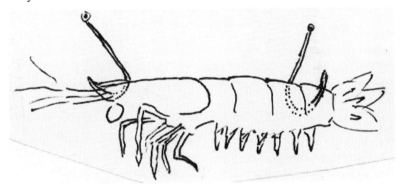

I find they cast better and stay alive longer if they're hooked through the tail as shown in the drawing. But hooking them through the head (avoid that dark spot or you'll kill the bait) is probably better for use under a popping cork.

For those unfamiliar with the popping cork, it's a type of float with a blunt end. After casting the bait and cork out into the water, you pull sharply on the line every 30 to 60 seconds. The cork makes a loud "Bloop!", the fish hear it and come to investigate, and there's your bait. They're quite effective.

If you don't care if the bait looks alive or is able to swim, break off the flapper on the tail and insert the hook point into the hole. Slide the shrimp as far up the hook as you can, and slide the hook point out of the underside of the shrimp. They will stay on the hook much better this way, and release quite a bit more scent. Redfish will smell them, even if the bait is down in the grass.

Dead shrimp work, so don't throw them away. Even frozen ones work, although probably not quite as well. Frozen shrimp are much harder to keep on the hook than live ones, a serious drawback to their usefulness as bait. They can always be used as chum, though.

-Crabs. We've already seen that reds will eat all kinds of crabs with little if any hesitation. They make a superb bait, especially for big redfish. The most commonly used bait crab for redfish is undoubtedly the blue crab, but any swimming crab you can catch will work. Large crabs can be cut into halves or quarters and used. Smaller, silver dollar sized live crabs make superb baits for big reds.

Live and frozen blue crabs are often available at bait shops. You can catch your own bait sized blue crabs with a long handled, fine mesh dip net by walking the shorelines of the lagoon and searching for them.

Possession of these crabs is a gray area under the law. There's a minimum size for blue crabs, but not all swimming crabs are blues.

Blue crabs have a nasty disposition and mean claws. Handle live individuals that still have those claws with a great deal of care.

For such an armor plated critter they're surprisingly delicate. Six or eight casts are usually all you'll get from a live crab before he bellies up.

Hook a live blue crab through one of its points.

Usually, people who've gone through the trouble of getting crabs use them exclusively for sight fishing, tossing them to reds they can see. If you want a bait you can just chuck out there and then let it do all the work of attracting the fish, you probably want to use some kind of bait fish.

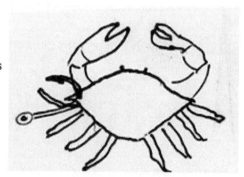

-Bait Fish. In the Indian River Lagoon three types of fish in four species make important bait sources for the redfisherman. Mullet, both black and silver, pinfish, and ladyfish all make superior baits. Other fish which can also be used effectively include killifish (mud minnows locally), pigfish, mojarra, pilchards, and menhaden (pogies locally). We'll concentrate on mullet, pinfish, and ladyfish. Anything you can do with them you can do with the other bait fish.

Silver mullet, often called finger mullet, are available from late in the spring until the end of the fall mullet run at about the end of October. Black mullet tolerate colder water temperatures and are available all year.

The silver mullet make an excellent live bait for redfish. Blacks tend to be large and are usually steaked or filleted and used as chunk baits.

Pinfish can be used live under a float or chunked. Because of their size ladyfish are almost always chunked.

One way to hook live minnows is through the lips (mullet, pinfish). Take the hook and drive it through the bottom lip and out through the top lip. Usually with mullet you insert the hook point into their mouth and out through the top lip. Another way to hook them is through the back or tail. You can hook almost any type of minnow this way. It works well when fishing the bait under a float. For pinfish this is the preferred method. Be careful to avoid the fish's backbone when you hook it.

Pinfish and mullet are usually caught with a castnet, although both can often be purchased live at bait shops. Frozen mullet are almost always available at bait shops. Ladyfish are usually caught with hook and line.

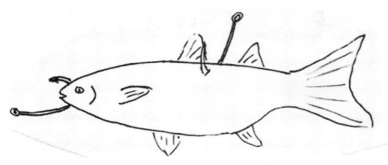

Dealing with live bait can be a real pain in the neck. It has to be obtained somehow, and then kept alive. This last is easier if you have a boat with a big live well, but not everyone does.

Live baits often won't stay where you want them, either. You cast them where you want them, and they swim away. Sometimes they are so lively that the target fish try to eat them, miss a few times, and give up. Enter- the <u>CHUNK</u>.

A chunk is a piece of baitfish, usually a steak but sometimes a fillet. It has several advantages over a live bait. You can catch bait to be chunked at your convenience and then keep it in your freezer until you need it. A chunk never swims away from where you throw it. Cutting chunks can turn a much-too-big bait into several perfectly sized baits. Redfish eat chunks with gusto most of the time, so don't be afraid to try one. Mullet, pinfish, and ladyfish can all be chunked.

When using chunks, make sure your hook is big enough. Don't try to hide that hook. Just put the hook in the meat and out through the skin (be sure no scales stick to the hook point), then cast the bait to where you know or think the redfish are.

Presenting the Bait– Still Fishing

No matter what kind of bait you use, it needs to be out in front of one or more fish if you have any hope of getting a bite. Are you sight

11

fishing, or still fishing and just hoping for a bite?

I have never truck fished since I've lived in Florida, but I see enough people doing it that I know they catch fish sometimes. Truck fishermen pull up at the water's edge, cast a line out, put the rod in a holder, and wait for a bite. They catch a fish if one happens to swim near their bait. They would catch more fish if they would cut up some pieces of fish and fling them out into the water around their bait, chumming if you will.

When I still fish (which is rarely) I always do it from a boat. Using a push pole I approach the area where I think or know there are some redfish, then anchor or stake out. I will take my bait, usually mullet, and cut up a half dozen or so into small pieces and fling them out where I intend to cast. Then I bait a couple of lines and cast them out into the now "sweetened" area. I wait 30 minutes maximum. If I don't get a bite I try somewhere else.

This is the simplest and most foolproof way of catching redfish that I know, and this one tip is worth the price of the book. If they are there you will catch them. The 30 minutes tells you if they are there or not, because if they're there it never takes that long to get a bite.

Presenting the Bait– Sight Fishing

For the sight fishers, redfish in the IRL have learned that a big "plop" anywhere near them is bad news. If you want to scare fish on the flats, hit them right behind the head with a nice juicy mullet chunk. Heck, flies put to close to redfish scare them when they're on the flats, never mind something that hits the water like a boulder.

Another presentation that will usually spook redfish is the "attacking bait." A common presentation error is casting past the fish and drawing the bait towards it. Fish aren't usually attacked by their prey, and in IRL waters they will seldom stand for it.

This book is incapable of describing every possible situation that you might encounter. Redfish lay up, tail, fin out, or cruise at varying rates of speed. They might be singles, in small groups, or be in a school containing hundreds of individuals. They might be stationary, or moving at a high rate of speed.

Regardless of what the fish is doing, most have what we can call a "strike zone." A strike zone is an area around the head of the fish where, if the bait is placed with skill, the fish will take it. Strike zones are almost always in front of the fish, and in their path of travel. The farther you ask the fish to move to take whatever it is you are offering, the less likely they are to take it.

Try to anticipate where the fish is going and put your offering there. Cast out in front of the fish. This is usually easier said than done, even for big groups of fish. The tendency of most fishermen is to cast to the fish, or to a swirl where the fish was a moment ago.

In order to make a cast to where the fish is going, you have to be able to see the fish and determine its speed and direction of movement.

Then you have to make a cast that lands far enough in front of the fish that it doesn't spook, but close enough that it's able to see your offering. The farther ahead you lead the fish, the more likely it is to change directions, not go where you cast, and never see your offering. Sight casting is a more challenging game than still fishing.

When you're fishing with bait, you can cast your offering in front of the fish and just leave it there. They will see and/or smell it. If they are at all on the feed one of them will usually pick it up. If you're throwing to a single this still holds true, but your target area is much smaller, since you have to put the bait into the strike zone of that individual.

Casts that are too long can often be saved without reeling the bait into the fish and spooking it. Start reeling before the bait hits the water. Hold the rod high and reel fast enough that the bait stays on the surface, where you can see it (very important!). When it gets to the place you want, stop reeling and let it sink (or swim, if it's alive).

This approach will still spook fish, but nowhere near as often as a conventional retrieve. This also works well for fish that are tailing, or laid-up fish. More than once I've had a fish I didn't know was there blow up on a bait that I was skimming across the surface, intending to put it in front of another fish that I could see. Needless to say, this is very surprising and tremendously exciting.

For most bait fishing my recommendation for hooks would be the Eagle Claw Kahle hook with the bronzed finish, #L141. I use these in sizes 2 (for standard shrimp), 1 (for large shrimp and small live minnows, chunks), 1/0 (larger minnows, crabs and chunks), and 2/0 (for still bigger

This redfish was fooled by a shallow running DOA Bait Buster, a soft plastic mullet imitation.

chunks) for any fish up to about 30 pounds or so. The wire is thin so they rust quite readily. I would like to think this helps the deeply hooked fish get rid of them more quickly, but honestly I don't know if this is true or not.

For large redfish I prefer circle hooks. My favorite is the Daiichi Circle Wide in sizes 6/0 through 9/0. While fish can still be gut hooked with circle hooks most of the time this style will catch in their lip.

Fishing With Lures

Lures are more convenient than bait. You don't have to keep them alive, or cold. They don't get stinky (mostly). You can put a bag of jerk baits and a few hooks in your pocket and off you go, ready to do battle. You can keep a box of lures in your vehicle along with a rod and reel and you are ready to go fishing 24/7. There are times when lures work better than does bait. Lastly, some folks appreciate the challenge of fooling fish with a piece of wood, metal, or plastic.

While everyone has their favorite lures, most experienced anglers would probably agree that you do not need a bazillion different lures in order to catch redfish anywhere, and certainly not in the IRL. So what I present here are those I carry. Different people will tell you different things. Find what works for you and use it.

An angler looking to put together a starter kit for redfishing in the IRL needs a variety of lures that can cover the entire water column, from the surface to the bottom. It's usually better to have several of each

The Rip Tide Weedless Jig, sadly now discontinued, was an excellent bait which works easily through most weeds, even through the manatee grass so common in the lagoon. Owner makes a similar product.

lure that you know works than a wide variety of stuff that just attracted your eye. The following chart offers guidelines.

Lure Recommendations for IRL Redfish

Lure Type	Uses
Surface Plug (popper/ chugger, stick bait)	Blind casting, especially when surface activity is observed. I don't like plugs but there is no substitute for a popper sometimes. Popular choices in surface plugs include the venerable Zara Spook, the MirroLure Top Dog series, and the Chug Bug from Storm. There are many other good ones. Disadvantages- hooks hang up on floating grass/weed, and make unhooking fish very difficult sometimes unless barbs are pressed down.
Spoon	A 1/4 ounce weedless spoon in gold or silver is a must in every redfisherman's kit. Captain Mike's and the Johnson Minnow are popular styles.
Jigs (1/8th to 3/8 ounce)	Jigs will take every species of gamefish in Florida waters. For maximum versatility get jig heads without tails and use these with a variety of soft plastic tails. Owner markets a weedless jighead that is extremely useful when used on grass flats.
Soft Plastics	An entire book could be written about using various soft plastic baits. You need to carry some to be used with jig heads (curly tails, grubs, and shad tails). You'll also need some twitch baits (Capt. Mike's Flats Candy 2, Bass Assassin, Sluggo, Jerk Worm, etc.). There are some plug-like soft plastics with single hooks that are excellent- the DOA Lure line (especially the Bait Buster and Shrimp) are especially effective redfish baits.

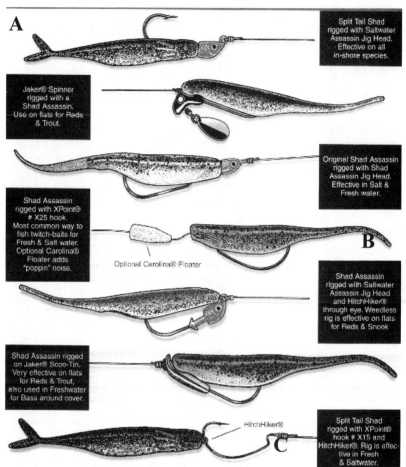

A — Split Tail Shad rigged with Saltwater Assassin Jig Head. Effective on all in-shore species.

Jaker® Spinner rigged with a Shad Assassin. Use on flats for Reds & Trout.

Original Shad Assassin rigged with Shad Assassin Jig Head. Effective in Salt & Fresh water.

Shad Assassin rigged with XPoint® # X25 hook. Most common way to fish twitch-baits for Fresh & Salt water. Optional Carolina® Floater adds "poppin" noise.

Optional Carolina® Floater

B

Shad Assassin rigged with Saltwater Assassin Jig Head and HitchHiker® through eye. Weedless rig is effective on flats for Reds & Snook

Shad Assassin rigged on Jaker® Scoo-Tin. Very effective on flats for Reds & Trout, also used in Freshwater for Bass around cover.

HitchHiker®

Split Tail Shad rigged with XPoint® hook # X15 and HitchHiker®. Rig is effective in Fresh & Saltwater.

C

This Rigging Plastics chart is courtesy of T.J. Stallings and the TTI Companies. Riggings labeled A, B (without the sinker), and C are particularly useful in the IRL system. "C" requires a product called a Hitch Hiker, a small corkscrew like piece of wire that clips to the hook, available from the TTI Companies.

Presenting the Lure

If you read "Presenting the Bait" on pp.12 and 13 you already know my philosophy of presenting lures. When sight fishing, put it out in front of them and leave it there until you think they are close enough to see it. One of the reasons that the Bass Assassin is one of my favorite baits is that you can toss it out in front of a swimming fish, let it sink to the bottom where because of its rigging it won't hang up in the grass, and just give it the tiniest twitch to catch the attention of the redfish as he/they approach it. Actually, you can do this with almost any weedless lure. It's deadly.

If you're blind casting then you need to cover water, the more the

Steven Perry and Alex Kumiski got this redfish double on DOA CAL jerk baits.

better. My guess is that the majority of fishermen approach fishing the flats by blind casting. Faced with a large amount of water, they tie on a lure that they hope will work and start throwing it. When there are a lot of fish around this actually works pretty well. When the water is high or dirty, or the wind is up and/or the sky is overcast you don't have much choice. You can't sight fish effectively under these conditions.

What lure should you use for blind casting? There is no single answer to this, but it ought to be something that you can throw a long way. It also should make noise, or have a lot of flash, or both. If there are a lot of baitfish in the water, more or less imitating them (especially in regards to size) is often a good idea. Since mullet are a primary forage, the shallow running DOA Bait Buster is an excellent lure. Surface lures often work well. A weedless spoon likewise is a good choice. I'm not a fan of plugs, but a rattling plug also makes sense if the water is deep enough or grass-free enough to allow its use. A shrimp-tipped bucktail jig, while neither flashy nor noisy, has the scent factor going for it and can also be very effective. What you want to do is let the fish know there is something there that they might be able to eat. You want to attract them to the lure.

Where should you direct your casts? If schools of bait are present, pepper them with casts. Redfish will cruise around and under bait schools. Any protruding structure, such as rocks, oysters, stumps, etc. deserve a few casts. Spoil islands and docks likewise make good targets all through the lagoon system. Drop-offs and sand bars need to be worked. The edges between grass beds and sand holes, and those sand holes themselves, offer good targets. When the water is high enough to allow it, the shoreline itself

17

Alex Kumiski got this nice red on a chartreuse DOA Shrimp, the 3 inch model.

needs some attention, especially if mangrove trees are growing there.

Don't just pitch your lure mindlessly, and always keep looking to see fish. It doesn't make any sense to allow a good opportunity to slip by because you weren't paying attention.

One other consideration- it pays to have more than one rod rigged when blind casting. Often the lures used for blind casting are flashy and noisy. If you do spot a fish, the sudden increase in noise in his neighborhood that results from a well placed cast may cause him to vacate the premises, pronto. Effective sight casting lures tend to be much more subtle than good blind casting lures. Keep at least one of each rigged up so you're ready for any situation that comes along.

Flies for IRL Redfish

Flies can be broadly divided into two general groups, the imitators and the attractors. Imitators are best used in sight fishing situations, when you can see the fish and place the fly in front of it. Attractors are best used in blind casting situations, where you have to attract the attention of the fish because conditions prevent sight fishing. The following list consists of both types. So let's take a look at the essential 10 redfish flies, starting with the imitators.

1. The Clouser Deep Minnow. It works everywhere, on a wide variety of fish. Since redfish often prefer to feed down on the bottom it's an excellent fly for them. You'll need a variety of different colors. If you think in terms of light, dark, neutral, and contrasting you'll be fine.

You'll also need a variety of sizes and weights. At the small end a size 4 with bead chain or micro lead eyes is good. At the large end a size 1/0 with 1/36th ounce lead eyes will sink like an anvil for those rare occasions when you need something like this.

Lastly, and this will be true for most of the fly patterns that follow, some of your Clouser Minnows need to have weedguards. My own prefer-

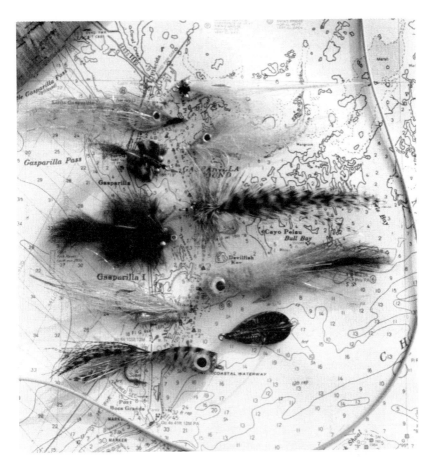

A good selection of redfish flies will include, from the top, Clouser Deep Minnow, Bendback, synthetic minnow, crab pattern, Seaducer, bunny strip fly, woolhead mullet, Rattle Rouser, Dupre Spoonfly, and a popper.

ence these days is for a double mono prong, but use whatever you're most comfortable with.

2. Bendbacks. Sometimes redfish are in very shallow water. When the water is only a few inches deep you need something that hits the water delicately and sinks slowly. Enter the bendback.

Like the Clouser Minnow, a variety of sizes and colors is needed. I have been known to wrap lead fuse wire around the hook shank in order to make these flies sink faster. I carry bendbacks as small as number 4 and as large as 3/0. These are excellent patterns to wing with synthetics.

If you tie your own, be careful not to bend the hook shank too much, a common error when making these flies. The shank should only be bent five degrees or so.

3. "Minnow" patterns from natural or synthetic fibers. The best known

natural fiber minnow is Lefty's Deceiver, although Joe Brooks's Blonde series works as well. But synthetics are really the material of choice for these flies.

Examples of this type of fly include slab flies, 3-D Flies, Enrico Puglisi's flies, Polar Fiber Minnows, and Sexy Flies. These flies can be tied in any sizes from tiny to huge and always remain easy to cast since they shed water so well.

4. Crabs. Redfish love crabs, and they eat all kinds- swimming crabs, mud crabs, fiddler crabs, horseshoe crabs, and more. You need a few faux crabs in your fly box.

My own favorite crab patterns are the Merkin (sizes 4 and 2) and an unnamed pattern that's like a sandwich made with felt and Furry Foam in the same sizes. As a rule redfish crabs don't need to be terribly realistic, only suggestive, and most should sink with some degree of expedience.

Live crabs are usually brown, tan, green, or some combination of those colors. The crab imitations you carry should reflect this.

As a rule crab flies need to be fished very slowly. You usually don't see live ones zipping around at high speeds.

5. Shrimp Flies. The one I use, have used for years, and will continue to use until I find a better one (not likely), was developed by Homer Rhodes in the 1930's and was called the Homer Rhodes Shrimp Fly. Most folks nowadays call it a Seaducer.

You can tie a Seaducer in any color combination you want, and in almost any size. All the variations are effective. But if I want it to more or less imitate a live shrimp, I tie it in either all natural grizzly, or grizzly dyed tan. I use these in sizes 4 through about 1/0. Sometimes I will tie in lead eyes, and some I leave unweighted. As in all the flies discussed so far, an added weedguard is often in excellent taste.

6. The Bunny Booger. Although this simple tie looks like nothing in particular, it has dynamite action when in the water and suggests a wide variety of redfish foods. I usually tie these in only sizes 2 and 1, always with lead eyes, either 1/50th or 1/36th ounce. My favorite colors include black, purple, rust, olive, and grizzly.

7. Woolhead Mullet (siliclone). These are time consuming to make and difficult to cast. Why carry them? When the fish are keying on mullet nothing else will do.

You can tie these in any size you like, as mullet do get large. When this fly gets large, though, casting it becomes nightmarish. I carry these in sizes 2 and 1, in grey and in white.

Sometimes the water is deep. Sometimes it's dirty. Sometimes there are clouds, or wind. And sometimes you have a combination of these factors, factors that prevent you from sight fishing. So you need some flies that call the fish to them by one means or another. We call these attractor patterns...

8. Rattle Rouser. These are bucktail streamers tied hook point up on a long shank hook. They can be unweighted or tied with lead eyes, as you prefer.

It's a good idea to carry some both ways. Tied underneath the hook is an epoxy coated, braided Mylar tube, inside of which a plastic or glass plastic worm rattle is inserted.

As you strip the fly the rattle makes an audible clicking sound, which attracts the attention of the fish. I don't use these very often but when you need it there is no substitute.

9. Dupre Spoonfly. Purists may be offended, since the Spoonfly is really a fly rod lure rather than a fly. I guess it depends on how you define "fly." Anyhow, these look like miniature Johnson Minnows, and work much the same way. A curved Mylar sheet coated with epoxy, Dupre's invention casts easily, hits the water lightly, tends to not twist your line, and is extremely effective. I'm not sure if the fish find it by vibration, flash, or both, but they certainly do find it.

Dupre makes his Spoonflies in a variety of colors. I've never noticed that any one works any better than any other.

10. Popper/Slider. Surface flies are not the best choice for redfish in most situations. However, as an attractor pattern when sight fishing conditions are poor they can be outstanding. The strikes are so exciting that a few less seems like a small price to pay.

I generally prefer using poppers when blind casting, since the commotion they make rings the dinner bell for quite a distance to a hungry fish. But sliders frequently work better in very shallow water where the noise of a popper can spook the fish. It pays to carry both.

These flies can be made of balsa, cork, clipped deer hair, or plastic foam. I generally prefer foam or deer hair, perhaps because I find them easiest to make.

There are lots of different designs out there. Use the ones with which you are most comfortable.

Lots of anglers carry poppers that are bigger than they need to be. Big poppers are not fun to cast, so use the smallest one you think will work. I generally carry them in sizes 4, 2, and 1, and seldom desire larger ones.

I believe that it's the sound that irritates fish into striking surface lures of any kind, and color is relatively unimportant. Feel free to disagree with me. Use whatever color you think works best!

Whether you tie your own or purchase them from a tier or fly shop, these flies will put fish on your line anywhere, anytime.

As far as presentation goes, I've beaten that subject to death already. Please read "Presenting Bait" on pp. 12 and 13 and "Presenting Lures" on pp. 16 to 18. Approach the problem the same way.

Boats

If you accept the fact that boats are like fishing rods you'll find what follows easier to swallow. How are boats like fishing rods? Well, most serious fishermen have from several to a lot of rods. Each one has a specific use, because no one rod will perform all functions equally well. So it is with boats.

You don't need an expensive skiff to catch redfish. Ken Shannon and Maxx Kumiski are about to put the finishing touch on a fine Mosquito Lagoon red.

Hand powered boats (canoes and kayaks, HPB's from here on) are relatively inexpensive and fairly easy to store. Maintenance is usually a non-issue. Fuel costs, well there aren't any.

The down side of these boats is that they don't cover much water in a day (but a lot more than if you were wading), and you have to sweat to make them go. I don't find either of these issues much of a problem and own a little fleet of hand powered boats, from which I catch a lot of redfish.

If you have an HPB, don't try to make it into a skiff. The advantage of an HPB is that it can go where skiffs can't. Use the boat to its strengths and you will love it. Try to make it something it's not and you won't. Very simple, and good advice for any type of boat.

When I say skiff here I'm referring to any boat with an outboard motor, from a canoe with a motor mount to a Gheenoe to a johnboat to an Action Craft or other flats skiff. You can catch redfish from all of these. Whether it's an HPB or a $40,000 skiff, no boat does everything well. Whatever boat you have, you should try to use it to its strengths. When looking to buy a boat, buy one that does well what you prefer to do most of the time.

A good boat for redfishing should be quiet. It should pole (or paddle) easily. It should be able to float in shallow water. It should have space to store tackle, a rain jacket, an anchor, and your safety equipment. Space for a cooler is nice, as is a poling tower. You should be able to afford it.

The fish don't care what kind of boat you have, so if the vessel meets your needs then it's the right boat for you. The only way you can get a "righter" boat is to have more than one for different tasks.

Part Two– Geography, Biology, and the Changing Seasons

OK, I know some readers will skip this section. Big mistake. The geography of the IRL, the biology of the fish, and the changing of the seasons have profound impacts on redfishing here. The more you know about your quarry the more of them you'll catch. Ignorance has never been bliss.

Geography of the IRL

The IRL system stretches along the east coast of Florida between a string of barrier islands and the mainland. The north terminus is at (somewhat arbitrarily) Ponce de Leon Inlet between Daytona and New Smyrna, and the St. Lucie inlet at Stuart is the southern end. The system spans a distance of 156 miles. Other ocean access along the lagoon is at Sebastian Inlet and Fort Pierce Inlet and a set of locks at Port Canaveral that opens into the Banana River Lagoon.

Because of its unique geography the IRL is the only place in the world where you can sight fish for big redfish like this in shallow water. Sean and George Yarko were pretty happy when we boated this one.

Shawn Healy gets up close and personal with a small Mosquito Lagoon red. No, they're not all big ones. The bait was a soft plastic from Cotee, called Reel Magic.

The Mosquito Lagoon connects with the Indian River Lagoon through the Haulover Canal. The Banana River Lagoon, a natural arm of the IRL, connects with the IRL through the Barge Canal and at a natural opening at Dragon Point in Melbourne.

The system is between one and three miles wide and averages only three feet deep. The dredged Intracoastal Waterway, maintained at a depth of 12 feet, runs most of the way through the lagoon. With the exception of the ICW and various crossing causeways, the system generally consists of a deeper basin area which ranges from five to seven feet deep, surrounded by extensive shallow flats.

Mangroves, both red and black, are the natural vegetation along the margins of the system, especially in the southern reaches. As you get closer to New Smyrna the mangroves become smaller and fewer.

Historically there were extensive *Spartina* grass marshes along the IRL but they've mostly been lost to development. The same is true of oysters, which are quite rare except in the vicinity of New Smyrna.

Much of the lagoon system is landlocked and is essentially a large, salty pond. From Melbourne to about Oak Hill, tidal influence is negligible and has little effect on the fish, fisherman, or fishing.

From a redfishing point of view, you can find reds anywhere in the system. Fishing for reds is best in the north end, with many more and much larger fish. Although redfishing can be good around Sebastian and up into Melbourne, the best redfishing occurs in the Banana River Lagoon north of the Pineda Causeway, in the Indian River Lagoon north of SR 520, and in the Mosquito Lagoon all the way to Ponce Inlet.

Biology of Redfish *(Sciaenops ocellatus)*

The fish we call redfish are found in the Atlantic Ocean from Massachusetts to Key West and in the Gulf of Mexico from Florida Bay to Vera Cruz, Mexico. They are rare north of Chesapeake Bay and south of Vera Cruz. Most of their life cycle is spent inshore in estuaries or near shore just off the beach.

Redfish prefer to live near barrier islands. Along the Atlantic coast these barriers extend from the south end of Chesapeake Bay south to Jupiter Inlet, Florida. The fish typically spawn along beaches in the vicinity of inlets and passes. Currents carry the eggs shoreward. Once the eggs hatch, the larval fish move into estuaries and sea grass areas.

Juvenile fish live in bays and estuaries for three or four years, then in most places move out into near shore ocean waters to repeat the cycle.

Redfish tolerate a wide range of salinities, from 0 to 50 parts per thousand. They prefer the optimum range of 20 to 40 parts per thousand. Juveniles tolerate freshwater better than adults can. Adults want higher salinities, around the normal seawater range of 30 parts per thousand.

Reds can also tolerate a wide range of water temperatures, from 50 degrees Fahrenheit to above 81 degrees. Small reds can stand an even broader temperature range. All reds are sensitive to rapid temperature drops. In cold weather redfish usually move into warmer water, wherever they can find it.

Generally redfish spawn in the fall as daylight hours decrease to 10.5 hours and water temperatures start to drop. Ordinarily, mature adults move close to passes and inlets for this activity. Anglers can find them here during the spawn. Adult males may be as young as three years and weigh only six or seven pounds. Females mature later, at a minimum of four years

In South Carolina redfish are called spottail bass.

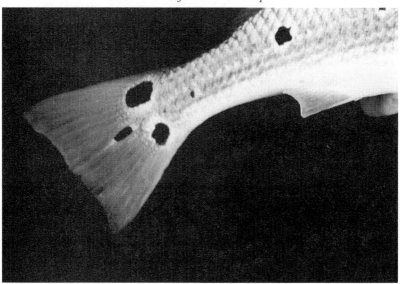

25

Jerk baits of all kinds make extremely effective lures for redfish. This particular bait is the DOA CAL. A three link section of bead chain was used for the eyes.

old and thirteen pounds. Most spawning fish are much older and larger than this, though. Adult fish throughout their range often exceed thirty pounds. Spawning activity occurs with the increased tidal flows around the full and new moons.

"Courtship" consists of males chasing females for three or four hours while drumming loudly and butting the females with their heads. Several males pursue a female simultaneously. Their coloration intensifies greatly during the excitement of the spawn. Just before dark the animals shudder and eject clouds of eggs and sperm into the water. These cells find each other by pure luck. A female may lay between two million and 60 million eggs in a single spawn depending on her size, and she may spawn more than once during the season. Clearly, releasing trophy fish benefits the long term health of the resource.

The fertilized eggs are tiny clear spheres measuring about one millimeter in diameter. Tiny oil globules inside the eggs keep them afloat. They hatch in 20 to 30 hours. The larval fish have an attached yolk sac for nourishment. These redfish larvae are quite sensitive to pollutants. If they hatch in water of poor quality they have little chance of surviving.

At the end of a week the larval redfish have absorbed the yolk sac and measure 2.5 millimeters long. They begin to feed on small plankton. If the water temperature drops below 68°F the larvae can no longer feed, so a severe winter following spawning may seriously affect the tiny fish. In the early larval stages, a salinity of 30 parts per thousand (normal seawater) is best. After the fragile early stage ends, changes in salinity usually cause no serious problems.

The larvae drift with other plankton for two to three weeks. Tidal currents transport them through inlets and passes into estuaries where they settle out along mangrove shorelines or in grass beds until the fins develop enough to allow swimming.

Young redfish grow rapidly under favorable conditions, about a half-inch per month. Although like humans each fish is a unique individual, redfish usually reach six or seven inches long and may be a foot long by their first birthday. At the length of eight inches the fish begin to school up. We call them "rat reds" at this stage in their life.

Larger fish continue growing rapidly, and although their length growth rate slows somewhat their girth growth rate increases. One individual, 26 inches long when caught, was tagged and released. After eight months in the wild it was caught again and measured 34 inches in length. Juvenile redfish live in estuaries, although they may leave for short intervals and move alongshore. At three to five years of age redfish generally move out of the estuary to a near shore school of adult fish.

Keep in mind there are exceptions to this behavior, with the IRL system being the best-known example. Here redfish mature and spawn without ever leaving the lagoon system. They provide anglers with a unique opportunity to sight fish for large, trophy sized redfish in a protected, shallow water environment.

Since estuaries are vital nursery grounds, deterioration or loss of estuarine habitats may seriously limit the number of fish that develop into adults. Redfish have been documented to live up to thirty years in the wild. As of 2004 the all-tackle world record redfish weighed 94 pounds, 2 ounces and was caught on November 7, 1984 at Cape Hatteras, North Carolina.

Although some seasonal migration of redfish occurs along the northern extreme of their range (from North Carolina to Virginia and back again), reds don't move around much according to several tagging studies conducted in Florida. Depending on where the studies were done, 50 to 85 percent of recaptured fish tagged in Florida estuaries were caught within six miles of the original tagging site. If you find redfish in an area today, you will find them there again in the future.

Redfish have what's called an inferior mouth (it's not of poor quality, it's on the lower side of their head). They're designed to feed on the bottom. Not surprisingly, much of their feeding is done there.

Although redfish feed opportunistically on almost anything they can catch with ease, they are particularly fond of both shrimp and crabs. I find crabs in the guts of more than half of the redfish I filet. These crab varieties include blue crabs, stone crabs, fiddler crabs, even small horseshoe crabs. I've found legs from large horseshoe crabs inside of redfish. Reds love crabs.

Reds use visual, tactile, and olfactory stimuli while feeding. In spite of popular opinion to the contrary they see quite well. They often key on their sense of touch or smell while feeding however, ignoring offerings lacking smell or tactile qualities. Redfish have tiny filaments at the end of their pectoral fins which are sensitive touch receptors.

Redfish sometimes become quite selective while feeding, keying in on a particular prey species and ignoring all other offerings. Although considered voracious feeders, sometimes they just don't eat at all. Please keep this in mind the next time your guide puts you on a bunch of uncooperative fish.

The Seasons of the Redfish

Like our lovely little planet, the redfish go through a yearly cycle. Their cycle doesn't follow the calendar, but rather the always changing length of daylight and ambient water temperature. It's a little different every year, because while the changing of length of day is a constant from year to year the weather is not. So what follows are generalizations.

Here in the IRL, beginning around November the fish get into their "winter mode." The adult fish, schooled up most of the time anyway, have finished spawning and stay mostly in the deeper basins (perfect weather days excepted), where they are hard to find. The juvenile fish, including those in the slot, tend to form schools at this time of year.

If the water temperature is dropping at this time of year the fish will be searching for thermal refuges and will be very hard to find. Days when fronts come through, or the day after a front, usually offer poor fishing for this and other reasons. If you luck out and find a hole full of fish though you'll have a day you'll never forget.

During sunny days when the water temperature starts to rise the fish will immediately move into shallow water. Shallow water warms faster than deep water. Also, the best fishing of the day will often be at sunset during the winter. The wind tends to lay down and the water has been warmed by the sun all day. Regardless of what the beginning water temperature is, if it rises three or four degrees you will find feeding fish.

All of the above assumes the wind is not howling. Redfish seem to not like the wind very much. I think they like the same kind of weather conditions we do, warm and sunny, with little or no wind. It's not that they won't eat when it's windy, because sometimes they will. But they seem to prefer beautiful, warm, windless days.

Another factor to keep in mind while winter fishing is that fish are cold blooded. I hear fishermen say, "They have to eat some time." Yes they do. But during the winter that time may not be today. Cold water slows their metabolism so they don't have to eat as often. When they do eat they seem to prefer smaller, lighter meals. Shrimp are a great winter bait, easier to digest than bait fish. If you're flinging artificials it might be a good idea to downsize. Smaller lures seem to work better during the cooler months.

Around April comes a discernable change in season. The patterns of the fish begin to change as the days lengthen and the water temperatures rise. Bait fish like silver mullet and pinfish start to appear. Good fishing can be an all day long affair now. Sadly, this action only lasts a relatively short time.

By the time mid-May arrives the summer pattern is established. Those slot sized fish, so plentiful and dependable during the winter, now become less predictable and harder to find. Prime fishing time frequently is over by the time the sea breeze kicks in. Lets look at a "typical" summer day on the lagoon system.

At dawn a light (zero to five miles per hour) breeze comes out of the west. There may be a lot of activity in shallow water– tailing fish, showering bait, the welcome sounds of gamefish feeding. As an angler you certainly hope for this! Somewhere around 9 or 10 AM what air movement there is dies and the water slicks out. It starts to get hot. Cumulus clouds start to build and make sight fishing difficult. Around 10 or 11 AM the breeze picks up, now out of the east as convection kicks in. This wind may quickly build to 15 MPH. At some point rain starts to fall out of the now towering clouds, huge sparks start flying around, and the prudent angler gets off the water if he hasn't already.

There have been many times when I've watched a flat, covered with fish in the morning, go dead as soon as the sea breeze kicked in. Sometimes you can watch the fish swim to the edge of the flat and drop off into deeper water. Getting an early start during the summer is frequently a critical component of angling success.

Because of the usually stable and predictable summer weather, it's the best time of the year to look for the schools of the big, adult fish. They are frequently in shallow water, near the surface with their fins out of the water, very easy to see. Furthermore, as summer comes to a close the adults sometimes form huge spawning schools with hundreds of fish, a bonus find for any angler.

The other event that occurs at the end of the summer is the start of the annual mullet run. Silver mullet are tropical fish and cannot tolerate the colder water temperatures of winter. So when the days shorten and the water temperatures begin to fall they school up and head south by the billions.

It's a banquet for every gamefish in the lagoon system, including redfish. The run typically peaks around the last two weeks of September and the first two weeks of October. Usually you look to find a mullet school with explosions occurring in it, and fish those. You might catch anything, but redfish certainly do shadow mullet schools and will make up part of the catch.

After the mullet run ends things quiet down a bit. Cold fronts start rolling through, and we're back into our winter pattern again. The earth has completed another cycle around the sun.

Part Three: Fishing Techniques

Shore Based Redfishing

This is the area of redfishing in which I have the least expertise, since I never do this. Shore fishing aficionados are typically truck fishermen, still fishing in a spot that's picked in a completely arbitrary manner, typically using big tackle and mullet for bait. Shore fishermen, whether they're fishing from the bank, a causeway, a canal, or a pier, cast a line out and hope a fish swims by. Sometimes it works, sometimes it doesn't.

The causeways across the lagoon system offer good places to do this type of fishing. The best are probably the Pineda Causeway across the Banana River Lagoon and the Max Brewer Causeway across the Indian River Lagoon. If I were going to fish this way I would stay near the land ends of the bridges on warm winter days, and near where the flat drops into deeper water on cold winter days or hot summer days. You may as well try to increase the odds in your favor.

The dike roads in the Merritt Island National Wildlife Refuge (MINWR) offer excellent access to those fishing from shore. Miles of roads snake along the shoreline of the Indian River and Mosquito Lagoons. Sometimes you can actually see the fish from these roads, so guess where you should set up shop?

I also see folks fishing from the banks of the Haulover and Barge Canals. In the Haulover Canal they definitely catch redfish sometimes, usually big ones well above the slot. I hardly ever see fish caught in the Barge Canal. I'd fish from the Pineda Causeway if I were down that way.

In the Sebastian area shore based red fishing is possible from either side of the lagoon. South of that there's shore fishing available, but reds are relatively scarce.

Remember that when you're shore fishing chum can make the difference between a mediocre day and a very good one.

Wading for Reds.

One of the most effective ways to approach redfish, as well as one of the most enjoyable of all the ways to fish, is by getting into the fish's element and wading. The angler has a low profile and keeps the disturbance of the water to a minimum, allowing him to sneak up on feeding fish without spooking them. It's possible to hook shallow water reds with literally just the leader out of the rod's tip. Exciting fishing!

For redfish wading in many situations will actually be more effective than fishing from a boat. In the lagoon redfish are heavily pursued by anglers in boats. The reds have learned that boats are trouble. Getting into casting range from a boat can be tough. A wading angler who tries to be quiet can literally get right on top of the fish.

On many days in the winter and spring, strong winds make even the most skilled boat handler want to scream in frustration. Fly fishing in

Barry Kent waded his way to a battle with this Mosquito Lagoon redfish.

particular is difficult when the boat is moving too fast because of strong winds. Many times it's hard to strip the line fast enough. A wading angler can fish in almost any kind of breeze.

In Florida during the summer months, shorts and some type of protective footwear are all that is needed for comfortable wading. I stepped on a flounder one time while wading barefoot, and although nothing happened as far as injury goes, the incident was all it took to convince me that some sort of shoe really was a good idea. Crabs, shells, broken bottles, and other hazards to the feet make barefoot wading a stupid thing to do.

The best footwear for wading are neoprene wading boots. These are similar to dive boots, but have a stiff plastic sole which give support and protection to the foot. Since they're ankle high, they also keep sand and shells out, and resist the suction effect that soft bottomed areas sometimes dish out. Take it from me- losing your shoe in bottom ooze in thigh deep water is not fun.

In the IRL system waders make winter wading possible. For those for whom wading is only practiced occasionally, the boot foot type of nylon wader will suffice. For those for whom wading is a way of life, stocking foot Gore Tex boots are the only way to go.

Stocking foot waders need wading boots. In our area, the hard

Wading works for redfish, as Maxx Kumiski and Mike Brown discovered

soled neoprene wading booties like those mentioned above work much better. You may need to purchase a second pair for use with the neoprene waders, a size or two larger than your shoe size, depending on what material the foot of your waders is made of.

Waders also need to carry all their paraphernalia. In the winter wading vests are a terrific way to carry tackle and accessories. Many excellent makes are on the market. Make sure the one you buy has enough storage space for everything that you'll need.

Often in the summer vests are too hot to be comfortable. The only thing to do is carry less stuff. Some fishermen carry extra lures on their hat, others carry accessories in an over the shoulder type of bag. Nu-Mark Manufacturing, a tackle manufacturer in Houston, specializes in accessories for the wading angler. Look for their products at your favorite tackle store.

What accessories will you need? This depends on the type of fishing done. Anglers using conventional tackle need extra lures, pliers, and a glove for handling fish as an absolute minimum. Material for making shock leaders, a stringer (see below), water, food, smoking materials (for those who indulge) etc. get added to the essentials. You can end up carrying a lot of "stuff."

Fly fishermen need more stuff. Although their lures are smaller, they need fly boxes, leader wheels, dry fly floatant, hook files, pliers, clippers, fish glove, and the usual miscellany as described above. Again, it can add up fast if care is not used. Be selective!

What techniques can waders use to find fish?

When you're wading it's hard to see fish because the angle between your eyes and the water surface is so small. However, if the light is good it can still be done. So what kind of lure do you choose?

If sighting conditions are bad you want an attractor type lure. For the bait fisherman a popping cork makes good sense as long as the depth of water permits it. Shrimp or pinfish make the best bait for this. DOA makes a rig they call the Deadly Combo, which has a three inch Glo Shrimp under a Cajun Clacker, and it is deadly.

A surface plug like a Chug Bug or a Zara Spook is always in excellent taste in this situation. Fan cast around yourself while you slowly work along the flat, covering as much water as possible.

A gold or silver spoon, or a shallow running DOA Bait Buster, or the Owner Bullet Jig #5146 (a weedless jig), are other good choices. You can cover a lot of water with these, and if you see any fish they make a more than passable sight fishing lure as well.

If sight fishing conditions are good then a more subtle lure is preferred. The three inch DOA Shrimp is a good choice, as is any of the various jerk baits. If I can see well and there are fish around I usually wait until a fish is spotted before casting. If you can't see well or if the fish are scarce, keeping the lure working is your best strategy.

If while wading down a flat the fish seem scarce, do what guides do and zigzag. Go in close to shore and then work farther out. The fish may be on the flat in slightly deeper or shallower water. By looking in different depths on the flat your chances of finding fish improve greatly.

Cast to any areas that you think might hold fish. Cast along oyster beds, rocks, stumps, pilings, docks, drop-offs, the edges of grassy and sandy areas, or any other area or structure that might hide a fish. In addition to increasing the odds for a strike, your targeting specific locations before every cast will improve your casting skills and this will pay big dividends on future trips.

Always look for signs of fish while wading. If fish are seen, try to get into the best possible position from which to cast. Sometimes you have to take any shot you have, but other times the fish are moving slowly and you can get that head on presentation.

Remember that the first cast is usually your best opportunity. Try to make it count. This is important. The first cast is always your best shot!

If you don't see anything after 30 or 40 minutes it's probably time to go try a different spot. Don't beat a dead horse. Rather, keep searching until you find some fish or it's time to leave.

Lastly, use care and common sense when wading. In our waters, stingrays are a cause for caution. Do the "stingray shuffle", never lifting your feet from the bottom. Kicking the ray's wing will cause it to swim away. Pinning it to the bottom will lead to a pierced leg.

In waters with sharks or alligators (and where aren't they?), dragging a stringer with fish on it is a huge invitation to trouble. And finally, although wading can be done as a solo act, safety considerations dictate that you fish with a buddy. So find another fishing maniac and go chase those fish together!

Your Hand Powered Boat

This section covers using both canoes and kayaks to catch redfish. Let's look at canoes first.

Nowadays, when flats boats have motors that could power airplanes and multi-thousand dollar price tags, when tournaments and competitions make fishing a pressure-cooker instead of an enjoyable, contemplative pastime, a canoe makes a lot of sense as a fishing craft for redfish. Why? There are many reasons. Let me go over a few.

First, canoes are versatile. There's no doubt that canoes can go many of the places that most other boats will, and a lot of places no other boats can.

Canoes are portable. Strap the boat to the roof of the car and go. You can launch it anyplace you can get vehicle access.

Canoes are quiet. Canoes never run out of fuel or break down. The aesthetic qualities of the boat are unequaled by any other type of craft except perhaps a sailboat, but it's hard to fish from sailboats.

Canoes are slow, but this insures working those likely-looking spots over thoroughly, instead of making only three casts, then heading off down the lagoon.

Paddling supplies exercise. Sometimes a little too much, when the wind is in your face and blowing twenty knots! But paddling truly is an excellent activity for the upper body.

Canoes require almost no maintenance. Whoever said that a boat was a hole in the water into which you pour money was not talking about a canoe. And the initial cost is low. It's possible to find high quality used canoes in the hundred to three hundred dollar range. They're a great first boat that you don't get rid of when you buy your second.

I am not an expert on canoe design, but I do know there are some real dogs out there. If the canoe is quite inexpensive new, it's probably poorly designed. You get what you pay for! Some of the better designs include those by Old Town, Mad River, Mohawk, and Sawyer. There are several others. If you intend to store the boat outside, stay away from ash gunwales and cane seats, as they'll rot. Also, many companies now use black plastic for its gunwales. These get unbelievably hot on a sunny day.

Concerning colors, fishermen want blue, grey, tan, or green. Avoid red and especially yellow. This is true of any shallow water fishing boat. The fish see these boats and spook at a much greater distance.

After purchasing the craft, it needs to be transported. Roof racks are a possibility, and the plastic foam blocks are another. Either works. If you opt for the blocks, make sure the slots cut in the blocks fit the gunwales of your boat. Attach two tie-down lines to one end of the canoe and a single line to the other. The end of the boat with two lines goes in the front of the car, the lines being tied to the corners of the bumper in an inverted "V".

The single line is tied in the back. I use "S" hooks to facilitate this tying to the bumpers. Use a single line or strap across amidships for added security. Do not use bungee cords, they are not secure!

The next consideration is paddles. Probably the most most popular paddle on the market today is made by Mohawk. They're durable, made of plastic and aluminum, and inexpensive. Although I personally don't care for them, most people who paddle with me like them and I own three.

It's a good idea to keep three paddles aboard. The extra one is an insurance policy against breakage through misuse, and an extra long paddle can be used to paddle while standing up, which is a help when sightfishing on flats.

Standing up while fishing from a canoe is not very difficult if you're at all coordinated.

For someone who likes to sightfish in shallow water, another good idea is a pushpole in the twelve to fourteen foot range. Mine is a14 foot, two piece ferruled pole made by Moonlighter, an excellent piece of equipment. It's used while standing, and gives better control of the boat when used against the bottom than the paddle can.

Purchase quality life vests as opposed to flotation cushions. It's the law. Believe me, the extra security you'll feel while wearing the lifejackets if caught out in some rough water will more than make up for the expense!

All boats need an anchor, and the canoe is no exception. An eight pound mushroom anchor attached to about fifteen feet of line will handle almost any Florida situation. I usually handle the anchor from the stern, simple personal preference.

Since your back and arms are supplying the power, your head had better supply the plan or you'll be doing a lot of extra work. If you're going out on a windy day, paddle into the wind before you start to fish. Paddle until you need a rest! Now you can drift the whole way back, taking it slow and easy, using the wind to your advantage. If you drift at first, the return paddle will seem incredibly long when you're tired after fishing all day.

A fact to face as a canoe owner, you'll be in the stern controlling the boat most of the time. A fishing buddy who knows how to paddle is a treasure. Two fishermen who know both fishing and paddling can switch ends periodically, each fishing, then controlling the boat in turn.

Earlier I mentioned standing while paddling or poling. There's a common misconception that standing in a canoe always immediately precedes going for a swim from the canoe. This is nonsense. Keep your feet well spread and you'll compensate immediately if the boat leans one way or the other. Further, the paddle or pole is used to help keep your balance. If you're concerned about it, first practice without your tackle in the boat!

To sum it up, a canoe is an inexpensive, low maintenance, reliable, versatile, easily transported, and effective fishing tool that is a joy to use if you enjoy moderate physical activity.

Kayaks have gotten lots of press as fishing craft over the past few years, and plenty of these wonderful little boats have been sold. Unfortunately lots of used ones are available because their owners purchased them without realizing how best to use them. Mastering any learning curve offers ample opportunities for frustration. My experience guiding fly fishers from kayaks has made this point extremely obvious.

Kayaks are small, silent, hand powered boats, originally developed by the Inuits for hunting seals. Since they're small, silent, and used for hunting, they absolutely excel at stalking skinny water fish of all kinds. I own two canoes and a "no wave slap hull" flats skiff. None of those vessels come close to the stalking ability of either of the kayak models I have.

Anyone who has spent any time looking at kayaks knows they come in two different styles, the sit insides and the sit on tops. While the choice of hull type is largely personal choice, I much prefer the sit on top type. Much kayak fishing involves wading. Getting on and off of a sit on top is much easier (and quieter) than getting out of and into the cockpit of a sit inside.

You choose a kayak in a fashion somewhat similar to the way you choose a fishing rod- any given model is better for some applications and not so good for others. On the boat rack in my yard are two different kayak models. One is long and thin and paddles easily. It's wonderful for those times when I need to cover long distances. The other is shorter and wider. While it doesn't paddle nearly as well I prefer it as a fishing boat because I can easily stand up in it, something that's impossible in the other one.

Ideally, also like fishing rods, you would have several different kayaks to cover different situations. Unfortunately for most people this isn't practical. Buy your boat so that it does well what you do most of the time. And never, ever buy one without water testing it first.

Spin or plug anglers can buy all kinds of accessories to make their boats more fishable. Rod holders, paddle holders, and livewells are a few examples. Fly fishers however (and dealers won't like my saying this) want none of this stuff. Line management is a primary concern of any fly caster

Allen Wyatt used a kayak to get this no motor zone redfish.

anywhere, and the more gadgets you have the more hang-ups there are for your line. Keep it clean and simple and you will be much happier.

I fly fish almost exclusively out of my kayaks. In addition to my paddle, rod, a single fly box, water, and required safety gear I carry a loop of bungee for securing the paddle to the boat when the paddle is not being used, a rope from the stern to my waist for towing the boat while wading, and a push pole or stakeout pole.

Most of my fishing occurs around the Kennedy Space Center- the Mosquito Lagoon, the Indian River Lagoon, the Banana River Lagoon. I see many kayakers out there, and most are making a fundamental mistake- they are using their boats in the same places that I'm using my skiff. When you do this you are not playing to the strengths of the kayak.

In spite of the claims of the manufacturer, my skiff needs 10 or 12 inches of water to float without scraping bottom. Usually I'm a little deeper. There are a few skiffs that float shallower than does mine, but I think it's safe to assume that any given skiff is going to draw more water than any given kayak will.

To make the best use of a kayak you need to go where skiffs can't. It's that simple. Do this and the chances of finding happy, hungry, stupid fish increases dramatically. No motor zones are one obvious application, but large areas of very shallow water (especially if there are lots of islands to break the wind) are another, often overlooked. If you fish where the pressure is light you have a distinct advantage. Sweat equity could be a kayak fisherman's single biggest weapon.

One disadvantage of kayaking is that your head is close to the water, making it hard to see. How do you locate fish?

Typically I'll get in water that's just deep enough to paddle easily and cruise at a fair rate of speed, looking in shallower water for signs of fish- wakes, tails, backs, busts. In other words, I cover water fairly rapidly, looking for fish or clues that tell me fish are there.

Once I've found some fish, if the bottom is hard I'll get out and wade. I can see better this way, I can hold the rod, and casting is much easier. I can silently stalk the fish I've found. More importantly, once I'm in position to take a good shot it is easy to stay there.

If the bottom is too soft to wade, but still deep enough to float the boat, I take my stake-out/push pole, three or so feet long, and use that to slowly maneuver the boat into casting position. It cannot be stressed too strongly that you must get into position to take a good shot. One good shot is worth dozens of mediocre ones. By using the pole to move the boat I can hold the rod in my casting hand and silently stalk the fish I've found. More importantly, once I'm in position to take a good shot it is easy to stay there. I just poke to pole into the bottom and hold it.

If the water gets too shallow to float the boat and you're scraping the bottom then even the pole is ineffective. Then I use the best tool of all, my fingers. Use your hands to push or pull the boat into position. Once in position to take a good shot it is easy to stay there. You might be stuck but if not just poke your digits into the mud.

You could use the paddle, but it requires two hands to use. You can stop in the proper position once you reach the spot where you want to be, but then you take time and risk making noise while putting the paddle down. You take more time picking up your rod. It's difficult to maintain your position if there is wind or current. If you lose your position you have to put the rod down, pick up the paddle, and go through the stalk sequence again. It simply doesn't work as well.

I will get on my knees and use my hands to pull the boat through mud, trying to get into a good casting position. If you're willing to do whatever it takes to quietly put the boat where it needs to be you will catch a lot of fish. You may be covered in mud at the end of the day, though.

All of the above assumes that you're sitting in your boat. What if you can stand?

I used to use my paddle to push or paddle the boat as circumstances dictated while standing in my kayak, looking for fish. When I spotted a fish I would have to bend down, secure the paddle, pick up the rod, straighten up, and try to find the fish again before I could cast. All this time the boat might be moving due to wind or current. It worked, but not particularly well.

One day I tried using a six foot long piece of ¾ inch PVC pipe as a push pole. Oh yeah, that was better. I could pole the boat with my left hand while I held the rod in my right (casting) hand. When a fish was spotted the response was almost immediate. If the bottom was soft (and where I fish it usually is or I would be wading) I could just poke the pipe into the bottom. I could hold it to maintain my position, or let it go if needed. If I

The author paddled into the no motor zone for an encounter with this typical slot sized redfish.

floated away from it I still had the paddle and could always go back and get it. Again, a dowel would work as well. It might work better, since a dowel can't fill with mud. If you use a PVC pipe you should plug or cap it somehow.

How close can you get to shallow water fish while in a kayak? Assuming you're being quiet (meaning absolutely silent) your average cast will be something in the order of 30 feet. Your fly, lure, or bait must land exactly where you want it to, but if you're a decent caster at that distance it's not usually a problem, even while sitting. It's not unusual for me to flop the fly at fish with only four or five feet of fly line out of the rod, and I frequently catch them. Honestly, they never know you're there.

If you follow the advice given here you're going to hook fish, and some days you'll get lots. What happens then depends on what kind of fish they are. Slot reds aren't going to give a huge battle. While fishing from a kayak you usually won't hook giant fish. You're fishing in two to six inches of water! But frequently the fish's back is out of the water and often times you are so close to them you can almost see every single scale. The intimacy of the stalk is thrilling and is the main reason I find this type of fishing so appealing.

Use the techniques described above and watch yourself rocket up that learning curve. You'll catch more redfish when you maximize your kayak's effectiveness.

Redfishing from a Skiff

Here's the scenario- two anglers have a boat, and have begun fishing in the Mosquito Lagoon, in which neither have fished before. Do they have any chance of success?

It depends on how hard they search. A situation like this often requires extensive hunting. Many tips follow which will hopefully make the hunt a more successful one.

Begin the search by moving fairly rapidly, looking for any signs of life, especially bait. An area showing obvious signs of life will much more likely hold fish than a location which otherwise looks good, but has no bait.

It's also important to work different types of areas until you find fish. Lee shorelines, open flats, sand bars, drop-offs, the back side of spoil islands, the front side of spoil islands, the ICW channel, and more, are all locations that could hold fish. Work them all in succession, using common sense to guide your search.

For example, don't try the windy side of an island with the wind from the north and the temperature in the fifties. A more likely location on a day like this would be a mud-bottomed, wind-sheltered south facing shoreline with sunshine warming the shallows. The fish could maintain a comfortable body temperature here, and could be persuaded to eat. The windy side of that island might be good on a warm day. The wave action oxygenates the water, and blows baitfish against the windward shoreline.

Search aggressively! If you don't look you will not find anything. This can't be stressed enough. If you want to find fish you have to look for them. Sometimes they just fall into your lap, but that's sheer luck.

Birds have long been used by savvy anglers to locate fish. Anytime terns start diving and screaming, it's easy to figure out that fish are underneath, piling into bait. However, in the lagoon system these fish are seldom reds.

Wading birds such as great blue herons or great egrets also feed on baitfish. Anytime several of these birds work together in one area, they indicate the presence of bait. Most of the time redfish will be there too, and sometimes the birds and the fish play the bait off of each other. Congregations of wading birds can certainly mean more than simple aesthetics.

Keep in mind that in shallow water of the lagoon system an outboard motor spooks fish from a long way off. Please keep your approach quiet and treat others with respect.

If you spend much time looking, whether you're in a kayak or a $40,000 skiff, sooner or later you're going to find fish. We have discussed earlier in this work how to present your bait, whatever it may be. Single fish are pretty straightforward, and when you find one you either catch it or spook it. If you catch it great. If not, look for another one.

But there are often large schools of redfish in the lagoon system, schools with a hundred or more fish in them. Let us discuss how to approach one of these schools of redfish.

A big school of fish has disadvantages as well as the obvious advantages. The schools has lots of (hopefully) hungry mouths, but it also has lots of eyes, ears, and lateral lines. All the fish in the school usually react as a unit. If you spook one, they all spook.

Regardless of the size of the fish in the school your approach should always start in more or less the same way. You want to silently position yourself between the fish and the sun so you can best see them. This is very important. Sometimes (not very often) the fish are moving fast and you don't have time to do this. Sometimes (again, not very often) they're crashing bait and their location is so obvious that your position doesn't matter. If the situation is such that you have to take whatever shot you can, do it. If you can, take the time to get between them and the sun.

The fish have a comfort zone, usually about 40 to 50 feet out from them. If you stay this far away and you're quiet they seem to not be bothered by your presence. If you get inside of this comfort zone they know you're there, and they usually respond by moving away from you. The temptation when they start to move away is to chase them. Hold that thought while we discuss fish moods. Then we will come back to the chase.

The fish have moods. While everything that affects them can't be considered, obvious factors include wind speed, water temperature, dissolved oxygen, boat traffic, fishing pressure, and where the fish happen to be located physically. When a school of redfish is happy there will be individuals at the surface with their tails and dorsal fins sticking out of the water. These fish aren't tailing! They're just laying there or lazily swimming, apparently enjoying the sunshine.

When a school of redfish is something less than happy, they will

While fly fishing, Mark Marsh got a dozen fish like this one from a single school by using a relaxed approach. Notice how nice the weather was.

A school of happy redfish is a beautiful thing. These fish are not tailing. Their fins are poking into the air because their bodies are just under the water's surface.

often be near or on the bottom. You won't be seeing any fins. They're still catchable though.

OK, back to the chase. When the fish are located along a bar, or along a shoreline, or in a slough, many times they won't want to move away from it. If you cause them to move away your best strategy is often to do nothing other than watch and wait to see what they do. Frequently they just move a short distance and stop. Give them a minute or two and they go back to doing whatever they were doing before you interrupted them. Even on a large flat they will often do this, especially if the weather is nice.

If you chase these fish aggressively all you succeed in doing is convincing them to leave. However, if you continue to approach these fish conservatively, giving them a chance to relax before you try again to catch one, you can frequently stay on a school for hours. Take it slow, and let the fish relax, and you will have a much better success rate with them.

Most of the time a large flat has no particular structure for the fish to key in on. If you get them moving they won't stop. You can't keep up with them with a pushpole, and if you use an electric motor they won't bite. If they're the only game in town try to stay with them from a comfortable distance and hope they stop. A lot of the time though, those fish will be gone for the day. That's when you say, "Man, they're in one of those moods." Yes, they are. That's fishing for you.

All things considered though, day in and day out you will catch more fish from a school if you take a very conservative approach to how you approach them. This is true whether you use bait, lures, or flies.

Of course it's possible, and desirable sometimes, to combine skiff

This is the same school of fish about 30 minutes later, steaming out towards deep water. Their demeanor is noticeably different.

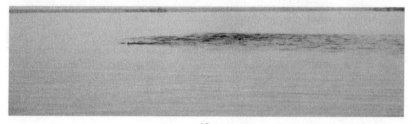

fishing with wading, or skiff fishing with a hand powered boat. Some days the fish won't let a boat near them. Their comfort zone on those days is so large you cannot get into casting range. If the bottom is hard enough for easy wading* it's often a good plan to back off of the fish, anchor the boat, and go wading after them. You'll never get a lot of fish by doing this, but you'll usually get one or two. One is so many more than none!

You can carry or tow canoes or kayaks to areas that are simply too far from an access point to paddle to, or that in order to paddle to would require a long, dangerous open water crossing. Frankly I'm surprised that more of this is not done.

*If the bottom is soft you can't move quickly or quietly enough to make this work. If you can stake out the boat with the pushpole's point then the bottom is too soft for easy wading.

Mr. and Mrs. Gene McDonough with a nice pair of IRL redfish, caught from a skiff. Holding a redfish by its jaw this way is not in the best interest of post-release survival.

This fish is nearly ready for release. The angler is holding the fish by the tail. When the fish wants to go, the fisherman won't be able to hold it. Notice that the bottom is sand here. The fish can't get tangled in grass. See p. 75 for more information on how to handle and release redfish.

Part Four: Where Are They?

There's a lot of water in the IRL system. Much of it seldom if ever holds redfish. As stated earlier in this work, with the exception of the area around Sebastian Inlet, the best redfish producing areas in the system are the Banana River Lagoon north of the Pineda Causeway, the Indian River Lagoon north of the SR 520 causeway, and the entire Mosquito Lagoon. One of the best areas is encompassed by the Kennedy Space Center, the Merritt Island National Wildlife Refuge, the Canaveral National Seashore, and the Canaveral Air Force Station. This area, over 200,000 acres, is mostly undeveloped land and protects the water and fisheries of the IRL, the BRL, and the ML.

Indian River Lagoon

Micco

US 1

Sebastian River

Shore Fishing
Most of the better shore fishing locations were already discussed. Please see pp. 30 and 45 for a review. Also, see the photos on the following pages for more opportunities.

Wading Opportunities
Excellent wading opportunities present themselves to the redfish angler in the lagoon system, in the IRL proper, the BRL, and the ML. First, the IRL.
South of Sebastian there aren't enough redfish to make a trip just for that. Snook, trout, and tarpon would make up most of a wader's catch.
On either side of the lagoon in the

This photo shows the west side of the IRL, across from Sebastian Inlet. The facing page shows the east side of the IRL from Sebastian Inlet south.

Sebastian area redfish can be found. North and south of the inlet off of A1A are wadable flats with excellent access. On the US 1 side there are numerous side roads off the US 1 that give waders access to the lagoon. Fishing is usually best early in the day here during the warmer months.

The shorelines of the IRL are developed, with little access other than at the causeways (no access allowed at the NASA Causeway) until you get north and east of Titusville. On the west side of the lagoon the only easy access for a wader without a boat is at the Scottsmoor boat ramp, at the end of Huntington Road in Scottsmoor. However, on the east side of the lagoon are a series of dike roads in the MINWR that give waders superb access.

A dike road runs along the northeast side of the IRL between US 1 and SR 3, north of the Haulover Canal. Another runs around Dummit Cove, from SR 3 to the Black Point Wildlife Drive, on the south side of the Haulover Canal. Yet another runs along the east side of the lagoon across from Titusville, starting on the south side of SR 406, wandering all the way down to Peacocks Pocket, and then coming back out to SR 406. I have caught redfish from all of these roads on many different occasions.

The roads aren't always open. Have a backup plan in case where you intend to go is closed.

Four pieces of safety information you need before wading off these roads:
-Never try to cross the ditch. The bottoms are muck, extremely treacherous.
-There are alligators. Pay attention, and don't tie caught fish to yourself.
-There are stingrays. Pay attention, and do the stingray shuffle.
-Never try to cross the ditch!

The bottom in some of these areas is soft, especially close to shore. It gets firmer as you get out a ways, unless you're in one of the "creeks"- Dummit, Catfish, or Gator. The bottom in the creeks is soft but wadable the whole way across.

Dike Road

Mosquito Lagoon

SR 3

Indian River Lagoon
Turnbull Basin

Dike Road

Black Point

Boat Ramps

This shows the north end of the IRL, at Turnbull Basin. The Scottsmoor Boat Ramp (the northernmost one in the photo) gives shore fishermen and waders a little bit of access to the west side of the lagoon. The dike road along the north-east of the lagoon gives much better access. Reach it off of US 1 or SR 3. The other dike road, lower down and to the right in this photo, is accessed off of SR 3. Look for the sign that says "L Pond Road." This is an ex-cellent area for shore fishing or hand pow-ered boats as well as straight wading.

The BRL has limited wading access. Along Tropical Trail on Merritt Island there are some places where you can get access to the west side of the BRL. This is an excellent flat and it is worth the trouble of finding access. You can also get access from the west side of the Pineda Causeway. The bottom in both areas is hard. I know how waders prefer firm bottoms!

The ML offers wading access in four areas. The first is along a dike road on the southwest side of the lagoon, accessible off of SR 3 (the Bio Lab Road) south of the Haulover Canal. The second is also on the west side, off SR 3 north of the canal at the WSEG boat ramp. This is limited access, but the area can be good in the winter. The third is on the southeast side of the lagoon at the Eddy Creek boat ramp, between Parking Lots 7 and 8 at Playalinda Beach, Canaveral National Seashore. The last one is also on the east side, at the north end of the National Seashore. There are actually several wading access points between Turtle Mound and Parking Lot 5 up there.

This dike road runs along the IRL on its east side, across the lagoon from Titusville. Access to this road is from four separate turnoffs from both SR 406 and SR 402.

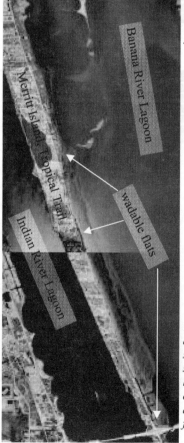

This is an excellent area for shore fishing or hand powered boats as well as wading. Sometimes you can literally see the fish from your vehicle as you drive along these roads!

Tropical Trail on Merritt Island gives waders access to the Banana River Lagoon. Look for single fish working along the shoreline, or schools of fish farther out. You may find very large fish here, but they are usually near the edge of the flat. That's the Pineda Causeway down at the very bottom, a good place to fish from shore.

48

Mosquito Lagoon

SR 3

Dike Road

Eddy Creek boat ramp

*The southwest side of the Mosquito Lagoon offers shore fishermen and waders ex-
cellent access from the dike road known as "Bio Lab Road." Access is from SR 3.
There as a small boat ramp here as well. Those wading will have to work, as the
bottom is fairly soft. Another access point is at the Eddy Creek boat ramp in Canaveral National Seashore. Waders would usually want to work along the south side of
the creek. The north
side is very soft, no fun
at all.*

Mosquito Lagoon
ICW

spoil island

boat ramp

*This photo shows the
vicinity of the WSEG
boat ramp, a small dirt
ramp north of the
Haulover Canal. Ac-
cess is to a small but
frequently productive
area, also good for
hand powered boats.
The bottom here is
fairly soft.*

49

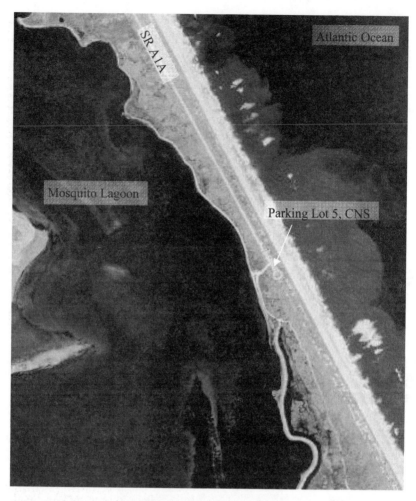

From the last parking lot in Canaveral National Seashore (coming south from New Smyrna Beach) you can wade either north or south with a good chance of encountering redfish. This is another good place to launch a hand powered boat.

Where to Redfish With Hand Powered Boats

It was stated earlier that the best use of hand powered boats is made when they're used where motor skiffs either can't or don't often go. Fortunately there are many such places in the IRL system. Keep in mind as you read this that you have a lot of flexibility where you can go. You can access almost all of the places the waders can, so read that section. Also, I'm not saying that you shouldn't or can't go where skiffs go. So read the section of skiffs too.

The Banana River Lagoon offers hand powered boaters two wonderful places to explore. One is the Thousand Islands area behind Cocoa Beach, accessed from Ramp Road. The islands offer fish a relatively safe

50

The Thousand Islands area of the Banana River Lagoon, behind Cocoa Beach. Another ramp on SR 520 across from the hospital gives access to the north side of this area.

haven from anglers in power boats, and you can sneak right up on them.

Secrets of Fishing the Banana River Manatee Refuge

You've heard the rumors about the giant redfish and other species in the "no motor zone." All of these can be found in the Banana River Manatee Sanctuary. But how do you get in there? And how, and maybe more importantly where, do you fish?

The next few pages detail all you need to know to fish the manatee refuge successfully. Follow the recommendations contained here, and you will enjoy some of the finest angling Florida has to offer.

No motors of any kind are allowed in the refuge. This means you can either paddle or row in, or use the wind. Remember however that sailboats function notoriously poorly as fishing boats.

Many people have said to me that they wish motors were allowed in there. I don't. The lack of motors is what makes this place so special. It's one place, in a rapidly growing state, where you can be close to an urban area and still feel like you're away from it all. The fact that boats with motors are not allowed make fishing there a relaxing, almost tranquil, and for me nearly religious experience.

Most anglers who fish the waters of the Refuge do so by canoe or kayak. When I use a canoe (either an Old Town Tripper or an Old Town Camper) I treat it as though it were a flats skiff, poling it with a two piece, ferruled fiberglass pushpole (made by Moonlighter Marine Products in Miami) while both I and the angler stand and search for targets to cast to. Sightfishing this way is tremendously exciting, and searching for fish in the crystal clear water combines the finest elements of hunting and fishing.

Canoeists also need paddles of course, and an anchor. The Coast Guard requires PFDs for all hands. The usual fishing needs are required, sunscreen, hat, sunglasses, dry box, pliers and hook file, maybe a cooler with snacks and drinks.

Kayaks are also excellent craft to use here. You can't stand up in most, but you can cover more area, since they paddle so much more easily. I use the Prowler, the Drifter, and the Scupper Pro models made by Ocean Kayak and find them all outstanding for this use.

This large piece of water starts about one and a half miles north of the SR 528 causeway and continues up to the NASA Causeway. Until Sept. 11, 2001 the entire area was fishable, but since them security concerns caused the east side to be closed. The west side is still open.

Unless you work for NASA or are retired military (in which case you can launch at KARS Park off of SR 3) access is at the north end of Banana River Drive, where it ends at the Barge Canal. Paddle across the canal and up the shoreline and you'll soon be there. In the NMZ you may see nothing, get into slot sized reds, or find a school of jumbos weighing over 30 pounds. This is not the place to try your ultralight tackle!

People often ask, "How far do I have to paddle if I go in the NMZ?" The answer to that really depends on you and the fish, and only God could answer it. Some days you literally won't make it up to the NMZ at all, there are so many fish on the flat south of there. And other days you'll go all the way to the NASA Causeway and will see only two or three fish along the way.

When I go to the NMZ, I stop as soon as I find fish, and I try to catch them. If I don't find any, I don't stop. It's just like any other fishing. If you fish where there aren't any, you don't catch very much.

Usually a day in the NMZ is a long, physical day. There's a lot of water. Sometimes the fishing is bad, and it's just a long, tough paddle. Other days it's spectacular, almost beyond belief, and you forget about the long, hard days.

If you enjoy paddling I highly recommend trying this spot. The only caveat I have, and it's a long one, is watch the weather. Please let me explain.

Weathermen are frequently wrong in their forecasts. Ordinarily I listen to the forecast, then go fishing anyway, even if a nasty day is predicted. The weatherman is wrong a lot! Makes sense! But the NMZ requires a long, open, unprotected paddle to the north. The reverse of that paddle must be performed before you can climb into the chariot and drive home at the end of the day. Any wind out of the south when you want to go

Captain Rodney Smith kayaked his way to this handsome no motor zone red, caught with fly tackle.

home and you're tired from fishing all day is painful, and if it's over 10 knots it's excruciating. I've been on some real survival tests up there and I no longer find them even slightly amusing. If the weatherman says, "Wind out of the south..." I won't go to the NMZ, end of story. There are other place to paddle.

If you intend to fly fish here a seven- or eight-weight rod with a floating weight forward line and plenty of backing is all you'll need. Bring an extra rod in its tube as a backup. If you break a rod when you're in fish and you don't have a spare you'll hate yourself. Ask me how I know!

If you choose spinning tackle, a ten or twelve pound outfit as described earlier in this book will work fine, as will comparable plugging tackle. Flies and lures have already been discussed, and nothing special is needed here. You're going to need lures with weedguards. The grass in the summer gets quite thick.

As already discussed, the fishery changes throughout the year. Winter is prime time for tailing fish, both redfish and black drum. The water level drops during the drier winter months, making the deeper flats where the really big fish feed wadable. On days with good weather you'll also find some really big trout up on the flats sunning themselves.

During the winter the best days are generally ones with settled weather, several days after the last front passed through. Light winds make for better fishing, especially if they're from the west, north, or northwest. A light northeast wind is also acceptable. You don't want any kind of a south wind at any time of the year, since you'll have to fight the wind at the end of the day when you're tired from fishing.

During the winter the best fishing is later in the day, usually after 4:00 PM (assuming a good weather day). The sun has warmed the water on the flats, which stimulates the appetites of our quarry.

Although there are no tides in the refuge, the best fishing days are usually (and this is a huge generalization) around the new moon. The fish seem spookiest and least cooperative around the time of the full moon. Other factors come into play though, which can affect this generalization.

As the days lengthen and the water warms, the black drum become harder and harder to find. The day comes when you'll start seeing more alligators than drum. It's time to shed the waders and shift into the summer mode. Due to the large numbers of 'gators (I often jest that they should have called it the Alligator Refuge) wading during the summer is not recommended. We seldom wade during the summer, fishing entirely from our boats then.

Since other parts of Florida have angling "slams", I've made up two for the refuge. The "Summer Slam" is a snook, a tarpon, a redfish, a seatrout, and a crevalle. No, it's not easy, but all these fish are there in the summer and it is a possibility. The "Winter Slam" is a trout, a redfish, and a black drum. You may as well have a goal before you go!

In order to get a summer slam, you'd better be prepared to put in a full solar day. Fishing can be quite good early in the day. Afternoon often brings thunderstorms. We typically wait these out at the side of the river, taking shelter in the brushy growth along the banks. After the storm passes we often have excellent fishing. It seems like the thunder and the cooling effect of the rain on the water in the river stimulate the fish to feed. We often fish until we can't see any more because of darkness.

The most important thing to keep in mind when fishing here is that there are no tides. Since the lagoon has no tidal flow, the fish cannot sit in the current and wait for food to come to them. And since big fish eat a lot, they have to keep moving. So what you know about where they were on any given day means almost nothing on a subsequent visit, even if it's the following day. Every day is a new hunt.

I usually paddle up into the refuge until I find some fish, often by

Patrick Phillips shows off a slot sized no motor zone redfish.

running them over. Then I get up and start poling, looking for fish. If you launch the canoe outside the refuge, look for fish while you paddle.

In the winter, in the morning, the fish will tend to lay up, sunning themselves. As the water warms during the day the fish will begin tailing, and get easier to see. You may also see (if you get really lucky) a large moving wave in the water caused by a school of fish.

When heading into the refuge in the winter you should wear chest high waders. Your shoes need plastic soles. You can work a batch of tailing fish much more effectively if you wade. The movement of the canoe puts out waves which the fish can sense, at which point they stop tailing.

In the summer the same basic strategy is used. The fish will be active in the morning, though. Look for redfish tailing or waking. Look for the schools of redfish pushing wakes.

You can wade in the summer, too. However, there are so many big alligators that I don't like to wade here then. Never keep a fish on a stringer and wade at this time of year!

This area is known for its giant (20-40 pound) redfish. Generally, the big fish school up and hang on the deeper parts of the flats, or on the edges of the flats. If you want to find them, that's where you must look. There are never any guarantees that you will find them. You go out and look for them, and take your chances. If fly fishing, use a fairly large fly for these big fish. Various types of soft plastics will work well, as will most natural baits.

Smaller redfish, to about 12 pounds or so, will work in very skinny water, sometimes with their backs out of the water along the shoreline. These fish can supply some very exciting fishing on lighter weight rods. Especially in the fall and winter, they'll look for small crabs along the shorelines. Crab flies are killers then.

Small minnows will often be pursued, too. Sometimes redfish will work in concert with snowy egrets and they bounce the hapless minnows between them. Always check out around feeding herons or egrets. Redfish often hunt in the immediate vicinity. For fly fishers the small brown Clouser minnow is best used in this situation, or a small soft plastic bait for spin anglers.

It used to be that you would pick which side of the river to fish by wind direction.* When fishing from a hand powered boat it was the single most important factor. Now that the east side is closed (I hope not permanently) you can fish the west side or not at all.

On the west side, access is at the Barge Canal at the north end of Banana River Drive, off SR 528. It's about a two mile paddle into the Refuge from here. Fish may be seen all along the flats here, too. If you launch here don't get tunnel vision about making it to the Refuge.

If you have a powerboat you're willing to risk to theft you can launch it at Kelly Park, on Banana River Drive south of 528, and tow your canoe up to the Refuge boundary. You anchor the boat and leave it there, then paddle up into the refuge. This is for the west side only, being unnecessary on the east side.

As you paddle up the west side there are a series of landmarks. The first is KARS Park. You may use this facility only with a retired military ID or an ID card available only to KSC employees. The park is at the edge of the no motor zone.

As you paddle north along the shoreline from here, you will come to a very small stream. A small flat surrounds the mouth of this stream, and often fish work here.

If you get out of the canoe here and stand on the bar looking east you will see a small PVC pipe in the water, out about 50-60 yards. That pipe marks the inner edge of a flat extending out about a half mile. In between where you stand and the inner edge of that flat lies a trough which runs north up past the next landmark, the radar station.

The flat often holds fish, including the schools of big reds. On lower water levels you can go out and find the outer edge of the flat. The flat itself has a grass bottom and is kind of soft for wading. The outer edge is a sand bar which is very easy to wade. Black drum often work out here in the winter, and a school of reds could come by any time. During the summer big jack crevalle run along the outer edge of this bar, which runs north for almost five miles.

Back along the shoreline, the next landmark is a large building with large satellite dishes mounted on it, and several antennae. Fish can be found all over the flat in front sometimes. The next landmark is a small point with a little cove behind it. Immediately to the north is the "bird tower", a microwave tower which used to have a large osprey nest in it. A small bar extends out from right in front of this tower, and a tiny stream enters the Banana River just to the north of it.

This entire area can be excellent. Off the point, in the little cove, on the flat between the tower and the point, on either side of the bar, and at the mouth of the creek should all be checked carefully. This is an excellent place to fish for reds at sunset.

North of here about one mile further another bar sticks out from the shoreline. To the north of this bar, out in the lagoon, you'll see an old bombing target. Against the shoreline here you'll see Buck Creek, a large shallow creek. Do not enter the creek. It's a restricted area and you can be arrested for trespassing. When the water is too low the fish will often be in the little basin between the creek and the bombing target. This basin is excellent for redfish and other species.

At this point we are about five miles north of KARS Park. Let's leave the remaining mile to the NASA Causeway a mystery to be explored by you, and turn our attention the east bank.

The East Side

*NOTICE! Due to terrorist events on 9/11/01 the entire east side of the no motor zone is closed to all entry. The east side includes all waters east of the marked channel. Trespassing here is a Federal offense! Hopefully it will open again someday soon.

On the east side access to the Refuge is by State Road 401 north of SR 528. Pull off to the left just south of the Canaveral Air Force Station gate. It's possible to launch a canoe here and paddle into the refuge.

Once you launch your canoe, head east along the power lines until you reach the shoreline. The shore is relatively featureless, but there's a nice grass bottom along here. This shoreline tends to be an all or nothing situation. If you see fish right away, you'll find them for several miles, up to a white (DANGER- NO TRESPASS) signboard in the water. If you don't see any right away, you probably won't until you pass a lovely copse of Australian pines with a little stream just to the north.

North of this a point sticks out into the river. There's a creek on the south side of this point. Again if the water is up, fish move in here.

The open part of the no motor zone stretches about seven miles along the west side of the Banana River. Launch at the barge canal and paddle north. You are not in the no motor zone until you pass the dayboards at KARS Park. ***Once you enter the NMZ you cannot legally go ashore for any reason.***

Note this little bump on the shoreline here is the small creek mentioned in the text, and...

...is the same one as here. The photo on the right runs to the north of the one to the left. The photo of the facing page runs still farther north. The NASA Causeway is about one mile north of the top of the photo on the facing page.

Inside this creek on the east side is a small dredge hole, which reds use in the winter. They may be cruising the shoreline of this creek too, again assuming sufficient water.

Once you pass the creek, if you head straight out into the lagoon from the point you will go over a large deep flat of which you may find the giant reds working. Winter brings black drum onto this flat. By heading west you will find a sand bar at the edge of the flat, just like we found at the edge of the flat on the west side of the river. This bar extends off to the

58

Buck Creek. This is a restricted area!

Duck Point

If you make it up this far you've paddled a fairly long way, especially of you started at the barge canal. The bar at the edge of the flat is clearly visible in this photo. If you want big redfish, this is the place to look, especially from Duck Point north, all the way to the NASA Causeway. Of course slot sized fish will be found here too, usually up closer to the shoreline.

south, almost to SR 401. It's a good place to look for reds and black drum. Continuing north, there are several points and coves. Any of these can have fish, and sometimes in high concentrations. You can only find them by looking. Shortly before you get to the line of spoil islands which extend out into the river you will come to another creek. This creek is deep and always holds fish, IF you are the first people there that day. Fish species vary by season. Large gators live here too. Expect to see them.

The line of spoil islands sometimes loads up with fish. At other times they are almost devoid of life. Again, you must look out here and see what it's like on the day you're there.

At this point you are about six miles from where you launched your boat. If you want to explore further, you are again on your own.

You now know everything you need to know to fish successfully in the Banana River Manatee Refuge- what to bring, when to go, where to look and what to look for, and how to get in. Keep in mind that although this may be the best fishery in the state, it's still fishing. If you don't catch some fish, try again. And if you don't catch any the second time, consider chartering with me! Good luck!

The Mosquito Lagoon at Oak Hill boasts a maze of islands and waterways. Much of the area is too shallow for motorboats, making it a paddler's delight. LeFil's Fish Camp in Oak Hill is just off the bottom of the photograph on the west side of the lagoon. The islands continue like this north to SR 44.

It was stated in the preceding section about the no motor zone that if the wind was forecast out of the south, then there were other places to paddle. For example, the Mosquito Lagoon's north end offers a maze of islands and waterways that don't require several pints of blood equity (as opposed to sweat equity) like the NMZ sometimes extracts. The downside of this area, up by Oak Hill and points north, is that you seldom find herds of giant redfish. But there are a lot of slot sized fish and it's a very pleasant day. It's fishable no matter which way the wind blows. Best of all, the motorboat traffic is usually light to non-existent because much of the area is too shallow for most motorboats most of the time.

There is some tidal influence here, with a range of about a foot. The tides run opposite to those at Ponce Inlet– if it's high at Ponce Inlet it's low at Oak Hill and vice versa.

Launch points to this area on the west side are at Lopez Fish Camp ($3.00 to launch at the time this was written) and at River Breeze Park (a wonderful facility), about a mile north. On the west side you can launch at Turtle Mound or at Eldora. There are more places to launch up in Edgewater and on the New Smyrna Beach side.

The approach here is the same as anywhere else. You paddle until you find a reasonable concentration of fish, then slow down and start fishing them. Don't start fishing until you find some fish!

Where to Redfish With a Skiff

Skiff fishermen, thank you for your patience, which will hopefully be rewarded right now.

Not all skiffs are created equal. The assumption here is that a skiff used for redfishing will need no more than 12 inches of water to float when fishing. You should never be running in water that shallow, and with all of the slow speed manatee zones we have now it's no longer legal to do so in most places discussed in this book.

Shallow water redfishing usually requires a pushpole. I know some guides who never use one, preferring to use an electric motor, but they tend to stay in deeper areas of about 18 inches or more. If you want to catch redfish you can use whatever you like but you had better be quiet.

For the trolling motor users, that means maintaining a steady, slow propeller speed to move the boat. Changing speeds alerts the fish to your presence, where a steady speed seems to bother them less.

Sebastian Inlet is an enormous fish magnet. One of the many species attracted to the inlet and its vicinity are redfish. Flats extend to both the north and south.

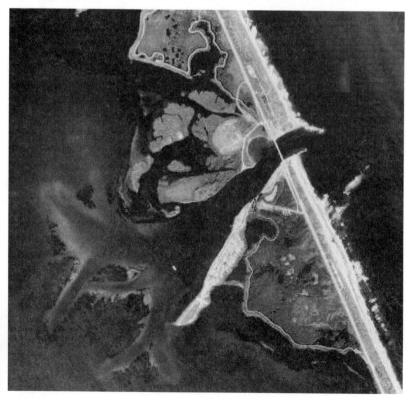

For polers, avoid grinding the pole on the bottom or banging it on the boat. The quieter you are the more success you'll have.

OK, where to go. Starting at the south, the area around and inside of Sebastian Inlet produces a lot of redfish. Don't get tunnel vision because there are a lot of other fish species here too. Flats north and south of the inlet on both sides of the lagoon will produce reds and other species as well. They are also found in small numbers around the spoil islands. The biggest reds will always be caught in the inlet itself. This fishing is usually best during the fall, especially when crabs are flushing on an outgoing tide.

Almost all the shorelines in this area are slow speed manatee zones. Enforcement is as rigorous as the manpower of the FWC will allow.

There are several boat ramps within 10 miles of the inlet. The closest one on the east side is at the Sebastian Inlet State Park (into the lagoon to the south of the inlet), and on the west side at Micco Marina, on the north side of the Sebastian River. There is a fee to use this ramp.

Moving north, the Banana River Lagoon has already been mentioned, especially the section between the Pineda Causeway and the SR 520 causeway. The area around the Thousand Islands (see p. 51) is frequently excellent, as is the west side flat running from the Pineda Causeway all the way up to the Cocoa Airport. In either place the fish could be singles or in big schools, or anything in between. Several line and tippet class world record redfish have been caught here, so don't be surprised if you find a lot of big fish.

This is an area that, when it's good, it's really good, and when it's bad it's horrible. If you try it here and don't find anything don't just write it off. If it wasn't good it wouldn't be in this book.

The photo on this page and the one on the facing page show the west and east shorelines of the IRL between SR 520 and SR 528, with 520 being just south of the bottom of the photos. Grass flats and residential docks are the main areas to fish here.

62

Ramps accessing this area include the ramp on Ramp Road in Cocoa Beach and the ramp on SR 520 across from the hospital. Another ramp is found at Kiwanis Park, north of SR 520 in Cocoa.

Again, much of this area is slow speed manatee zone, enforced by both the FWC and the Cocoa Beach Police Dept.

In the IRL the first section (the lagoon has been divided into these sections by the construction of the various causeways) to mention is that one between SR 520 and SR 528, a relatively lightly fished area with residences on both sides of the lagoon. Where waterfront residences are found so are docks (clearly visible in the photos), and these docks just load up with fish sometimes. The entire shoreline on both sides of the lagoon is a slow speed manatee zone through here.

If the recently passed hurricanes haven't blown them all down, there are a lot of trees along the east side of the lagoon here, protecting the shoreline from east winds. It's a good, protected area to fish under these conditions.

The closest boat ramp is a Brevard County facility on the southwest side of the SR 520 causeway in Cocoa. This is an excellent ramp, very protected from the wind.

If you were to run north under the SR 528 causeway you would be in the next section of the lagoon. Every year I tell myself I need to fish the southwestern side (south of the power plant in Sharpe) of this section more, and for some reason I never do it. It's similar to the section south, residences with docks.

Where I do fish is on the eastern side, between Pine Island and the NASA Causeway (see photo next page). Again, this entire shoreline is a slow speed manatee zone. And again, like anywhere you find redfish, sometimes there are none, sometimes they're scattered as singles, and sometimes there are herds of fish in here.

The south side of the NASA Causeway is a protected area to fish on a north wind, especially during the wintertime.

On the southwest side of the NASA Causeway is a nice little flat that I seldom fish. The manatee zone here extends all the way out to the channel. It's a long way in there at slow speed.

The nearest boat ramp to this section is a Brevard County ramp off

The photo to the left shows the west side of the IRL by the NASA Causeway. The shore-lines to the north and south of the causeway are rela-tively lightly fished, per-haps due to the large slow speed manatee zones.

NASA Cswy

US 1

The photo to the right shows the east side of the IRL, south of the NASA Causeway. If the water is clean this can be a very pro-ductive area.

Rinker Canal

Indian River Lagoon

Pine Islands

of US 1 at Port St. John, between the two power stations. It is very exposed to the east and tough to use with a hard east wind.

On the northwest side of the NASA Causeway is a nice area which holds fish but which in my experience is very incon-sistent. I have never seen a school of fish in here, only singles. It's a good place to check on a west wind.

As you head north here (on the west side) you come up to Titus-ville. I know that fish use this shoreline, especially all of the residential docks, but I never fish here. I prefer the aesthetics of the wildlife refuge's shorelines.

The east side of the IRL, across the lagoon from Titusville. This extensive flat supports lots of redfish and can be an excellent area. Peacocks Pocket is just off the photo at the top. The NASA Causeway is at the bottom. Both Banana Creek and Morse Creek are restricted, no entry areas. The dredge hole, used to obtain fill for the NASA Causeway, is clearly visible in the photo.

Speaking of which, let's look at the east side of the lagoon in this section. A large flat extends from the Max Brewer Causeway in Titusville all the way to the NASA Causeway. This is a very fishy area and produces a lot of fish. Again, both singles and schools will be found here. The bottom is very broken up, with thick grass and big white sandy spots. When the water is clear it's a beautiful place to fish.

Banana Creek is restricted, and no entry is allowed. It probably functions as a fish refuge because of this. There are frequently fish along the outside of it.

Morse Creek is not posted against entry. I was in there one time and a helicopter came, hovered about 50 feet over my head, and a soldier manning a 50 caliber machine gun (which he had pointed at me) motioned for me to get out. He got my attention and I've never gone in there again.

This entire area is (you probably can guess what's coming) a slow speed manatee zone.

There are two boat ramps convenient to this stretch of the lagoon. The first is a Brevard County facility at Kennedy Point Park, just south of SR 50 on US 1. This is an excellent ramp, protected in any weather. The other is at the Parrish Park, also a Brevard County facility, on the east side of the Max Brewer Causeway next to the FWC station. While this is an excellent ramp, it is exposed to a hard west wind, and launching and loading can be tough when it's 15 knots or better.

Parrish Park also gives the boater access to the IRL north. The section of the lagoon that the ramp in on is fairly small but does produce some fish. Just to the north and east of the ramp is a watersports area, heavily used by personal watercraft and windsurfers. Fishing is not recom-

Railroad Trestle

dredge hole

Indian River Lagoon

Titusville Marina

This flat is relatively lightly fished, but can be very productive if the water is clean.

mended here. Up by the railroad trestle fish are found sometimes, and it's a good place to look on a north wind.

The west side has some beautiful flats. I don't fish here as much as I should. It can be excellent if the water is clean.

On the north side of the Titusville Marina is a city park, where a hand powered boat can be dropped in to give access to this side. There is a very protected boat ramp at the Titusville Marina, maintained by the city of Titusville. There is also a fuel dock here (with typical fuel dock prices), one of the few anywhere around here.

North of the railroad trestle is the expansive Turnbull Basin. This area may have the best redfishing in the entire Indian River Lagoon. Along the west side a flat runs from the railroad trestle all the way to Turnbull Creek at the north end of the lagoon. On the east side a flat also runs from the railroad trestle all the way to Turnbull Creek, with three breaks in it. The first is at Dummit Creek, the second at the Haulover Canal, and the third is at Griffis Bay. Redfish, in singles or in large schools, can be found anywhere here.

The entire eastern side of this section between the channel and the shoreline, from the railroad trestle to the Haulover Canal, is a slow speed manatee zone. There is another slow speed zone on the west side up by Scottsmoor, and at the north end of the lagoon.

Boat ramps accessing this area can be found at Parrish Park, Titusville Marina, on Huntington Road off of US 1 in Scottsmor, and at the Haulover Canal off of SR 3 in the MINWR. All of these are public ramps. Cars sometimes are broken into at the Haulover and Scottsmoor ramps. All that's left to discuss in the IRL system is the Mosquito Lagoon. What can

Turnbull Creek

Griffis Bay

Dummit Creek

Turnbull Basin on the IRL. This area is a redfish factory. The same photo with different labels is found on p. 47.

one say about the Mosquito Lagoon? It's the premier redfish fishery on Florida's east coast. Flats encircle the entire water body, and all those flats

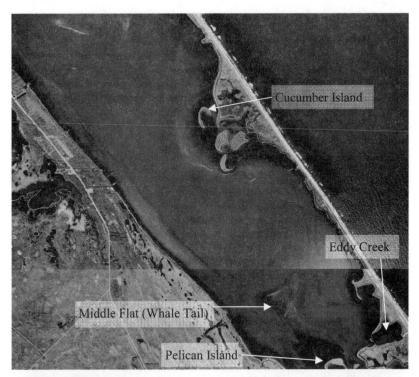

The south end of the Mosquito Lagoon. Consistently good areas include the Middle Flat (also called the Whale Tail), the Cucumber Island area, and the entire west side flat. Notice all the bars, none of which are well marked, and some of which aren't marked at all.

are capable of producing redfish, as singles or in large schools. Spoil islands and bars give some topography. The bars, few of which are marked, make navigation here more hazardous than anywhere else in the system. The saving grace that the bottom here is mostly sand with very few rocks. If you run aground you may get stuck, but you usually won't punch holes in your boat. Let's break the lagoon into three sections, and discuss those three pieces, starting at the south end.

For the purpose of this discussion, the south end of the Mosquito Lagoon goes from the actual south end north to the Haulover Canal. The entire flat on the west side may hold fish, sometimes in big schools, more often as singles or small groups. This is miles of fishable water. There are abandoned residential canals and docks along here which serve as structure that can concentrate fish.

On the north side of Pelican Island there's a large flat, the northern end of which is often called the Whale Tail because of its shape. This is an excellent area for singles and schools.

The entire east side may hold fish, both singles and in schools. An excellent area is found on the large flat west of Cucumber Island.

The central portion of the Mosquito Lagoon. The west side has a string of spoil islands to the west of the ICW. The east side has an enormous flat broken up by islands and sloughs. There are again many unmarked bars along the east side.

Boat ramps for this area are found at Eddy Creek, at Bio Lab Road off of SR 3, and at the Haulover Canal, also off of SR 3. There are no manatee slow speed zones here (yet).

The central portion is a little different. The Intracoastal Waterway runs up along the west side. When the channel was originally dug (an environmentally sound project, I'm sure), the spoil was piled up to the west of the channel. This produced a long string of spoil islands, sometimes called "clinkers" locally. These islands can hold fish on both sides, in and out, all the way from the canal up to Oak Hill. The manatee slow speed zone extends from the ICW west to the shoreline the entire way.

On the east side a maze of shallow flats, islands, and sloughs await. In much of this area once you shut down it's a long pole to get out, so be careful of where you go. Also, there are numerous unmarked bars at the edges of the flats that are very easy to run aground on, especially when the light is poor.

You will find redfish in all kinds of numbers configurations, from singles to large schools, all through here. One of the more consistent areas is the large flat inside of Tiger Shoal, which should be a poll/troll, no combustion engine use allowed area by the time this book is in print. This flat is so large that eight or ten boats can easily fish it simultaneously and hardly ever get in each other's way. I have seen a thousand fish at a time up here in five or six separate schools. It is never a bad place to check.

Another good place to look here is along the south side of Georges Bank. Single fish or big schools can be found here, and it is a well known hang out for big fish.

With the exception of the already mentioned manatee slow speed zone along the west side of the lagoon there is a 30 mph speed limit on all lagoon waters at the time this was written. Winds of change have been blowing, so that may change before long.

Boat ramps for this area are found at the Haulover Canal, the old Beacon 42 Fish Camp ramp off of SR 3 north of the Haulover Canal, the WSEG ramp, still farther north off of SR 3, and at River Breeze Park, a Volusia County facility about a mile north of Oak Hill off of US 1. Your vehicle is safest at River Breeze. Break-ins have been an ongoing problem at all MINWR ramps.

The last area in our where to go fishing tour of the IRL system is the north end of the Mosquito Lagoon. This area is completely different than any we've discussed. A confusing maze of islands and mostly shallow waterways extends from Georges Bank at Oak Hill north all the way to SR 44 in New Smyrna. A wonderful place for paddlers, I'm not about to recommend that the power boater who doesn't know where he's going should go zipping around here.

There is tidal movement to the water too. The inlet influencing the water levels here is at Ponce Inlet, north of New Smyrna Beach, so the water has a good distance to travel. Wind can have more of an influence on water levels than tide. Tides at Oak Hill are exactly opposite of those at the inlet, so if it's high at the inlet it's low at Oak Hill, and vice versa. The range is usually less than a foot, but it can be more than that.

There are a lot of redfish. For those who carefully wish to learn their way around, the ICW runs along the west side of this area, all the way to New Smyrna giving access to the west side for those who don't know their way through the maze. The entire channel is a slow speed manatee zone. On the east side is the "old channel" a relatively deep but not very well marked channel that gives access to the east side.

The are cuts that go across from east to west. The Shotgun cuts diagonally from the southwest to the northeast across the lagoon near Oak Hill. Slippery Creek, a winding and sometimes shallow waterway, runs from the south end of Bissett Bay to Eldora. Neither channel is marked. The Shipyard Canal connects the north end of the Old Channel to the ICW, running diagonally from southeast to northwest.

The best advice I could give to anyone wanting to fish this area

The north end of the Mosquito Lagoon is a confusing maze of islands and water-ways. Take your time when boating here if you're not familiar with the area.

from a skiff for the first time is to go slow, and fish shallows adjacent to the deeper areas first. When you start to get a feel for the place and you have good light and clear water so you can see where you're going, then it's time to explore a little more. Do that exploring early in the day so if you do get in a jam you have time to get out of it again.

There are a lot of fish up here, as always, in configurations rang-ing from singles to large schools. You can usually find somewhere out of the wind to fish.

The only manatee zone here is along the ICW.

Boat ramps for this area include Lopez Fish Camp and River Breeze Park on the west side, and the ramp at Turtle Mound on the east side. There is another ramp way up by the City Hall in Edgewater.

How sweet it is– Rusty Chinnis with a 28 pound, fly caught redfish from the IRL.

Part Five: The Search for Big Fish

Size matters, in spite of statements by certain pundits to the contrary. This is America, the land where more is better. So we all want to catch big fish. If you're fishing in the IRL system, especially that part between the Pineda Causeway and Oak Hill, you're lucky, because you're in Big Redfish Central. Nowhere in the world can rival the shallow water fishing we have here for big redfish.

Mind you, you can find bigger redfish in other places. Louisiana, Texas, and the Carolinas all produce redfish that are as big or bigger than IRL reds. But, because the unique geography here essentially landlocks our fish, we can fish for them in mere inches of water, where we can see them, cast to them, and watch them respond to our lures every step of the way.

What is a big redfish, and how do you go about catching them? In a school of adult fish in the area described just above, the average fish will be around 40 inches long and weigh about 20 pounds. You'll sometimes get a "little" fish (speaking relatively) of 30 or 32 inches. This is a young adult that just joined the school. At the top end they could be over 50 inches long and weigh over 40 pounds.

Like anything else in fishing, if you want to find these big fish you must look for them. They usually won't just fall into your lap, and you seldom find them in the same types of places where the schools of slot sized fish are found. For one thing, they prefer deeper water, between about 18 inches and three feet deep. For another thing, they're usually found close to deeper water yet. Any time you find a place where a bar or the edge of a flat drops off into five or six feet of water there's a chance that big redfish will use that spot. That having been said, I know of several places that look perfect, but I never see big fish there. No, I don't know why not. It's just one of those things.

Next, big fish practically demand nice weather. There has only been a handful of times when we went looking for big redfish with snotty weather and caught some. Your chances of finding and catching them are much better if the weather is nice.

If you enjoy fishing after dark (I don't) you can catch them at night. I went out with Karl Dienst one night south of the NASA Causeway. We used big, live black mullet for bait and caught several whoppers. The Haulover Canal also produces big reds after dark.

Big reds are usually found in schools (with the possible exception of the no motor zone). We've already discussed how to approach schools of fish, so you might want to review that.

Where does one go looking for jumbos? If you're in the Banana River Lagoon, the area around the Thousand Islands and the entire west side flat from the Pineda Causeway to the airport can produce. Also, the no motor zone is well known for producing giant reds.

Here's another happy angler with a jumbo redfish from the Indian River Lagoon.

The author and Bo Mantooth with a big Indian River Lagoon redfish.

In the Indian River Lagoon the entire east shoreline from Pine Island to Peacock Pocket can produce big reds, including the area around the NASA Causeway. The entire Turnbull Basin produces big reds.

In the Mosquito Lagoon, the Middle Flat often has big reds around it. On the east side of the ICW, across from the canal coming out from the

Bo Mantooth releases one, a different fish than the one above. I fished him and his father for two days, they did very well.

Beacon 42 Fish Camp ramp, is a large flat. The deep water around this flat sometimes has big reds on it. The deep side of both Tiger Shoal and Georges Bank sometimes gets big fish.

The Haulover Canal often gets big reds in it, especially at either end. This is strictly a bait fishing proposition.

That's all the places I know where you might find big reds. Of course you might get lucky and stumble into them anyplace, but if you intend to look for them those are the places to look.

What do you use for bait for these fish? They'll hit anything the smaller fish will. Jumbo shrimp, live or cut mullet, live or cut pinfish, live pigfish, or cut ladyfish all work well. For lures, some people enjoy watching them smash surface plugs. I don't like using all those hooks for a fish I have to release, so I prefer single hook lures. Jerk baits (the Bass Assassin is a favorite), the venerable gold spoon, or the DOA Bait Buster work well. For flies, different days demand different things. If you carry the flies discussed earlier in this book you'll have what you need to catch them.

Handling and Releasing Big Redfish

Let's talk about handling and releasing these fish. A 30 pound redfish is probably about 20 years old and is a tremendous resource for the lagoon system. If you handle this treasure carelessly it will die. If you handle it carefully it will survive, spawn and make baby reds for the future, and perhaps give someone else the same thrill it gave you. I wouldn't tell you how and where to catch these fish without also telling you how to handle

Patti Sunderland with a big redfish from the Indian River Lagoon.

Mike Barnett had been trying to get a 20 pound red on a fly for over 20 years. This one, weighing in at 23 pounds, did the trick.

and release them in good shape.

First of all, if you're using bait, set the hook with expedience. That fish is going to swallow the bait if you don't. Gut hooked fish die about half the time, even if all other release procedures are correctly carried out.

Next, fight the fish like you mean it. The less time the fish spends at the end of the line the more likely it is to survive being caught. See "How to Fight Fish" in a later chapter, p. 79.

Should you use a net? I'm not sure if this is good or not. I never use one, preferring to use my fingers. How?

First off, ordinarily it's a two man operation. When the rod man brings the fish is close to the boat, the other kneels down in the boat on the side the fish is on. Grab the leader with your dominant hand. Reach down and grab the fish in front of the tail with the other. Use a death grip! Reach under the chin of the fish so you can cradle it in the arm of your dominant hand, and gently lift it into the boat. Piece of cake!

The fish can no longer breathe, so work fast. If we're going to get photos I unhook the fish, put the Boga Grip on it, and immediately put it back into the water until we're ready.

What if the fish swallowed the hook? If you tear it out the fish will die. If you leave it in it might survive (that 50 percent chance is a LOT more than zero) so cut the line off at the lips of the fish and let it take its chances. A little prayer that it makes it can't hurt.

We've all seen photos of big redfish hanging by their jaws from a Boga Grip. Not only does this make for an extremely ugly photo, it is probably the worst thing you could do to the fish besides tossing it up on the bank, or into a cooler.

Fish live in a weightless environment. Their bodies are completely supported by the water, and have evolved with that support. You float in water, don't you? Look at how much more robust your skeleton is than that of a fish. You have to fight gravity.

When you remove a fish from the water their support is gone. Gravity is yanking at it. If you hold a fish vertically, all its guts slide down-hill, tearing tissues all along the way. It is a superior way to injure and quite possibly kill the fish.

If you look at the photos in this book, every fish but one is being held horizontally. In the photo at the bottom of this page, Mike Deegan is cradling the fish in the water. It makes for a great photo, and is so much better for the fish.

The most stable weather occurs during the summer, and that's when fishing for big redfish is usually best. The water temperatures are relatively high then, which means dissolved oxygen is low. Ordinarily the fish will need to be revived, sometimes for quite a while. Please take the time to do this.

Mike Deegan cradles a nice red he got on fly in the Indian River Lagoon. Mike was wading at the time he hooked this fish.

Lou Payor with a nice red he got from a canoe up in the no motor zone of the Banana River Lagoon. This fish was caught on a fly, a black Clouser Minnow.

To revive a redfish, keep it in the water. Use your thumb or a Boga Grip on its bottom jaw and move the fish forward, easiest to do in a boat by having someone use the trolling motor or the pushpole to move the boat forward, or out of the boat by walking in a circle. This forces water over his gills. When you think he's ready, grasp him in front of the tail, letting his jaw go, and rock him from side to side. If he is ready you won't be able to hold him. If not, go back to the thumb in the mouth approach. Keep doing this until he's ready to go.

There's one last thing you need to keep in mind about releasing any redfish, especially during the summer when there is less oxygen in the water. The grass on the bottom gets particularly thick during the summer. The fish, completely unnerved from its encounter with you and exhausted after fighting for its life, usually swims straight to the bottom after release, If there's grass there the fish will often burrow into it, apparently trying to hide. They get tangled up in the grass and they're too tired to fight their way back out, eventually going belly up and dying. If at all possible, let them go over a deeper area so they can get a head of steam up, or over a sandy spot for the same reason. More of your released fish will survive if you do this.

Catch and release works. Studies have shown that redfish hooked in the lip, when properly handled and released, have a survival rate of 96 or 97 percent. Please handle your fish properly and help maintain the superb fishery that belongs to the IRL system.

How to Fight a Fish!

Regardless of their size, fish to be released benefit greatly from a short, hard fight. Most of us can recall (even if it was way back there when we had physical education classes in school) over-exercising. The next day our muscles were sore and stiff, making it difficult and painful to move.

For most of us this was not a life threatening situation. But a fish played too long develops the same lactic acid compounds in its muscle tissue that we do when we over-exercise, and a fish that can't move well often falls prey to one of its many enemies.

Oxygen dissolves better in cold water than warm. While here in Florida we never find truly cold water, the cooler temperatures of winter often put more fight into the fish we catch, particularly redfish. Fish caught at this time of year suffer less stress because of the relatively plentiful oxygen supply in the water. Without having done any research on the subject, common sense leads me to believe that post-release mortality is lower during the winter months.

In summer, fighting fish hard is more important simply because the water has less oxygen. The fish is in a situation somewhat analogous to the marathon runner who trains at sea level and then has to run a race at 10,000 feet- there is simply not enough oxygen. Concerned anglers will fight the fish hard during the summer in consideration for their quarry, and bring the fight to a conclusion as quickly as possible.

Why else should anglers try to fight the fish hard? The least altruistic reason is that the longer the fight, the more likely it is that the fish will get away. The hook wears a larger and larger hole in the tissue and a brief moment of slack allows it to fall out. Abrasion on the leader leads to breakage. The angler tires, makes a mistake, and the fish breaks off. It just makes more sense for everyone involved to fight the fish hard and beat it quickly.

Let's take a look at seven general rules for fighting fish which hold for any type of tackle, and which lead to a higher success rate for any angler lucky enough or skillful enough to hang a big fish every now and then.

-Rule 1: Use the heaviest line that's practical. Why use six pound tippet if ten pound will work just as well? I take exception with anglers who tell me ultralight tackle is more "sporting". They may have more fun with it but it really beats up on the fish. I was speaking with a guide recently who told me that his client fought a 30 pound plus redfish for an hour and a half on fly tackle before the hook pulled out. My response was the guy should learn how to fight fish. The guide said he did a good job but was using six pound tippet. WHY?

Why would anyone chasing 30 pound reds use six pound tippet unless he was specifically trying for a world record? In my own saltwater fly fishing I seldom use less than twelve pound tippet, with the exception of bonefishing.

-Rule 2: Set the drag correctly. Whether using fly or spin tackle set the drag at 25% of the breaking strength of the line/tippet. To determine the drag setting get a good scale and tie the leader to it. Then tie the other end of the scale to a tree or some other immovable object. Point the rod directly at the scale and pull until the drag starts to release. The reading on the scale is the actual, measured drag setting on the reel.

-Rule 3: Learn to put maximum pressure on the fish. While we're still tied to the tree, start putting some bend in the rod while holding the reel to prevent drag slip. How much pressure can you put on the line before it breaks? Try this two different ways.

First, use the method already described, and second, try lifting a ten pound mushroom anchor off the floor while standing on a table. If you're a fly fisher, use twelve-weight fly tackle with 16 pound class tippet. Using the scale, with all their strength, the maximum pressure the most skilled fly anglers can put on that 16 pound tippet will be only twelve pounds or so. Similar results will be garnered with spinning tackle.

During a demonstration with a 10 pound anchor, several men in succession stood on a table and tried to use a 12-weight fly rod to lift the anchor. Most of us just barely moved it and it was the rod that broke, rather than the leader. The obvious conclusion is that with 16 pound tippet the average fly fisherman will never break the line no matter how hard he pulls on it, and with twelve pound tippet we can use 90% of our pulling strength and still be safe as long as we let go when the fish surges.

I've seen many different men try this with 12-weight tackle. Most of them only got the scale up to four or five pounds, and the highest I've ever seen anybody get it was 14 pounds. Don't believe me? Try it yourself!

While your neighbors might call for the men in the white coats if they see you fighting trees with your fishing tackle, if you want to learn to put maximum pressure on the fish you hook, few things are more valuable.

-Rule 4: When the fish swims away, don't try to stop it. While you can't pull hard enough to break a 16 pound class tippet, plenty of fish can. If the fish surges or makes a run and you try to stop it, something will break. While the fish runs it uses up its energy reserves. Let it go.

Snook fishing around mangroves or other structure provides one exception to this rule. If a fish runs toward the roots, you have a decision to make. If he gets in there, he's gone. Should you try to stop him? Every single time!

I once tried to stop a snook in the Everglades that I had hooked on a surface plug. I locked up the reel, trying to keep that fish from the trees. The eight pound test line went slack and the plug floated to the surface. I reeled it in and checked it- the hooks had straightened before the eight pound line broke.

-Rule 5: Either you or the fish should be gaining line. When the fish stops its run, you should immediately attack it and start gaining line. Never let up or let the fish rest. While neither of you takes line, he is resting. He recovers faster that you, so a standoff only prolongs the fight. Show the fish you want to win. Like Billy Pate said, "You have to want the fish more than he wants to get away, and the fish thinks he's going to die."

-Rule 6: Learn to use side pressure. In shallow water, or if the fish is at the surface in deep water, pulling up on its head does little or nothing to tire it or break its spirit. The fish spreads its pectoral fins and resists with almost no effort. If you pull to the side, or better yet pull down (the famous "down-and-dirty" move) the fish has no defense and has to use muscle power to overcome the pull. Furthermore, once it has been rolled over once or twice, the fish will give up more quickly. Always pull opposite to the direction the fish is moving. In other words, if the fish is moving to the left, pull to the right and vice versa.

Rule 7: Change the angle of pull frequently. This one is particularly important for lifting fish from deep water. If you maintain a constant angle of pull, the fish can easily adjust to it, spread its pectoral fins, and resist with minimum effort. If you change the angle of pull constantly by "wagging" the rod, the fish will usually come right up. He may go right back down again, but he has to work to do this, and thus gets tired. It is very important while doing this to have the butt of the rod pointing down at the fish rather than up at the sky. High sticking does not move the fish and leads to broken tackle.

Learn and use these seven techniques for fighting fish. You will catch more of the fish you hook, the fish you release will have a better survival rate, and those around you will know that they are in the presence of a world class fisherman.

This angler is applying side pressure to a big Banana River Lagoon redfish.

Practical Tips for Reds on Top

<u>Why?</u>

One of the most amusing and exciting sights in inshore saltwater angling occurs when topwater baits are used for redfish. The placement of this fish's mouth is what biologists refer to as inferior. No, it's not of lower quality, it's under the head and pointing down, much like a bonefish's. Redfish feed down, off the bottom, much of the time. So when they come up to the surface they often have trouble taking the bait. Hookups are somewhat less likely, but since you can see all the action the excitement level is much higher. So things sort of balance out.

Redfish, or red drum or channel bass if you prefer, are one of the most popular inshore saltwater gamefish from Texas to Virginia. I suspect that the majority of fishermen chasing reds use live bait, but not only are surface plugs much more exciting to use, but under the correct conditions they are incredibly effective as well.

<u>When and Where</u>

What are the correct conditions? The water has to be shallow. From about knee to waist deep is about right. In shallower water plugs usually spook the fish, although they'll still hit hair bugs and sliders presented with a fly rod. In deeper water the fish are usually down on the bottom, and that noise way up there is just too far away to be bothered with.

In other words, oyster, sand, or mud bars, mangrove shorelines, or mud and grass flats are all prime locations for throwing top water baits. Wind conditions seem to be relatively unimportant. In general, on calm days use a quiet plug, and on windy days use a noisy plug. Let's take a look at various types of surface baits.

<u>The Baits– Conventional</u>

We can take all those saltwater surface plugs out in the tackle store and roughly divide them into four basic categories. First are the "stick" plugs, a simple design exemplified by Heddon's Zara Spook. The Rebel Jumpin' Minnow, YoZuri's Banana Boat, and Bagley's Jumping Mullet are other excellent examples of this type of plug. These plugs cast very well, but have little if any built-in action. They depend on the angler's rod manipulation to entice the fish. Although it takes some practice to learn that retrieve (a zigzagging motion known as "walking-the-dog"), fishermen who master it will take a lot of fish, and not just reds. Trout, snook, and tarpon also aggressively attack these plugs. This type of lure is best used when the wind is light and the water surface smooth. They get lost when there's a lot of wave action.

The second type come equipped with propellers. These come in a variety of different shapes, but two of the most popular are Rhoden's Johnny Rattler and the Devil's Horse, manufactured by Smithwick. While these designs have never been among my personal favorites, many of my friends use them with great success. Again, these lures require some degree of angler manipulation for maximum effectiveness. Because of the noise the make, they work well in windy conditions.

The next type are the floater-diver minnows like the Rapala and the Rebel. While not strictly surface plugs, these can be slowly worked on top around structure such as fallen trees or oysters in shallow water, then retrieved more rapidly for a subsurface retrieve the rest of the way. This feature makes them particularly effective around channel edges and other types of drop-offs. The greatest advantage of these lipped minnow-type plugs is that they have built-in action and so are easiest to use. Their main disadvantage is their relatively low density and high wind resistance, which makes them a poor choice on windy days or when long casts are necessary.

The last type are the popper/chugger designs. Although each design has its proponents, I prefer these types. My favorite is Smithwick's Carrot Top. Unfortunately these plugs are no longer made. I've found some other good ones though, including Storm's Chug Bug, the Yozuri Hydro Tiger, and the Rebel Pop-R. These lures cast a long way, and make a lot of noise. As you might have guessed, these characteristics make them excellent baits to use when the water surface is rough.

These types of lures can be used as "fish-finders". Knowing that the noise the plug makes will draw your quarry from a considerable distance away, you can use them to find fish. I've seen it happen often enough to know that it happens regularly!

Sometimes you will see a wake approaching the plug from a considerable distance, and the adrenaline explosion in your body can only be matched by the one that occurs when the wake and the plug finally get together. It's heart-stopping, especially when the fish is the fifteen or twenty pound range.

Another lure type which needs mentioning here are the soft plastic baits. DOA manufactures a lure called the Bait Buster, a mullet imitation. While the shallow runner sinks when at rest, it can be retrieved right along the surface and results in explosive strikes. Furthermore, it has only one hook, an important consideration in today's world of catch and release angling.

Most of the soft plastic jerk baits can be worked at the surface, too, and have the advantages of having a single hook that cab be rigged so that it's almost completely weedless. Some of the better ones include the RipTide Jerk Bait, the Bass Assassin Saltwater Shad, the Cotee Reel Magic, and Captain Mike's Flats Candy series.

The Baits– Fly Rod

For fly fishers there are fewer options as far as fly design goes. Here are the choices:
-the SLIDER. Sliders have a pointed face, and therefore make very little noise. Their main attraction to the fish is the wake they create on the surface. They're best used when the water is calm and very shallow, a situation

where a noisy lure would spook the fish.

-the DIVER. These float at rest and dive when retrieved. The Dahlberg Diver is the best known of these flies. These are wonderful choices when the water quickly drops off from shallow to deep, in areas such as oyster bars, or on days when the fish seem reluctant to take on the surface. You can attract their attention by popping the fly a few times, then dive it underneath with a steady retrieve. The bubble trail these flies leave seems very appealing to a wide variety of gamefish. Another trick is to use these divers on a sinking line. This gets it down, and gives it an action achievable in no other way. Of course then it's not "on top." Pardon my digression.

-the POPPER. These have a blunt face and pop and gurgle when retrieved. These are my personal favorites, especially for wading, when actually seeing fish is difficult due to the low angle of your eyes to the water. I've always felt that the more of the fish's senses you can appeal to, the better the chances of a strike. Poppers appeal to both sight and hearing, and again, are good choices when it's windy and the water is rough.

These flies are made from deer hair, plastic foam, balsa wood, cork, and many other materials. What you choose depends of your personal preference and what's available. I like both deer hair and foam, and tend not to use cork and balsa. Certainly the floatability and durability of foam fly rod lures is unmatched by any other material.

Techniques

Regardless of the type of lure preferred, here are some tips for using them. The first is to keep the bait moving. Redfish are not largemouth bass; they have no interest in a stationary lure. If a red follows the bait and doesn't take, continue at a steady pace or speed up the retrieve, rather than slowing down. If you slow down, the fish will usually veer off and won't take. They may not take when you speed up, either, but the odds are much better that they will.

Second, when a redfish commits to the lure, he usually (80-90% of the time) eats it. Short strikes are almost always caused by a fouled lure, most often when the hooks catch some floating grass or other debris. Short of modifying the plug by changing the hook arrangement, there's nothing to be done about this but to clean the hooks off and try again. At least you know that there's a fish out there, and that it's interested.

Reds, especially when in very shallow water, may have a hard time getting the bait in their mouth. Again, surface lures may not put as manay fish in the boat as other types, but the visuals frequently make their use worthwhile anyway.

I find that if there's a lot of grass floating, short casts are more effective, simply because the plug doesn't have as much time to foul before it gets cleaned off again. Sometimes there is so much floating grass that there's no other choice but to use jerk bait or a sub-surface bait!

Third, use a loop knot to attach the lure to the line. I use the no name loop knot. The loop gives the bait maximum freedom to swing and

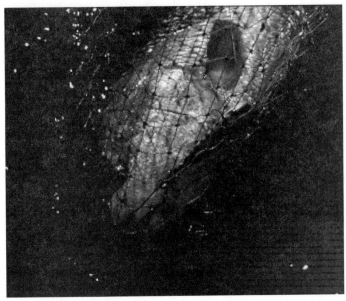

This red nailed a popping plug.

sway, especially if a shock leader is used. Never use a snap or a swivel. Not only are these pieces of hardware unnecessary, they adversely affect the action of the bait.

Next, if the water clarity permits, try to actually see some fish before beginning to cast. Look for tails, wakes, cruising fish, or best of all, fish attacking bait. It may take some time to locate them, but you will always fish harder and with a lot more confidence if you know there are fish in the area where you're casting.

Lastly, experiment some to see which plug and retrieve combination works best for you. Oftentimes, when I fish with friends, we'll both be throwing the same lure. One person usually outfishes the other. I think the major reason for this is minor variations in our style of retrieve; the fish for some reason find one retrieve with that particular bait more appealing. So develop a relationship with your favorite lures. You'll catch more fish with them that way.

Other Considerations

In addition to the excitement of watching the fish attack the lure, there are other advantages to using surface baits for redfish. You never have to buy, catch, or handle live bait. Getting hung up on the bottom becomes a thing of the past. Catfish seldom hit surface plugs. What I like best, though, is the number of other desirable species that will eagerly eat a top water bait. Seatrout of all sizes hit them with a vengeance. Snook, jacks, bluefish, tarpon, ladyfish, even mangrove snapper, have all been taken while plugging for reds.

So try fishing for redfish on top, and watch the excitement of fishing for reds just explode!

Last Word

Well, you've made it to the end of the book. Thanks for reading it!

If you're a fisherman and not a member of the Coastal Conservation Association you really should join at your earliest opportunity. The organization isn't perfect, but it's one of only a few looking out for the interests of recreational anglers. You might not agree with everything they do, but when you disagree with something the government does do you leave the country? CCA has been a tremendous force in improving Florida's (and other states) coastal fisheries for the last 20 years or so.

The forces aligning against recreational angling are organized and well financed. As an individual you can't do much about Marine Protection Areas and other results of junk science, but as the member of an organization you have some political clout. It's sad that we have to think and act this way, but if we don't defend our own interests we can be sure no one else will do it for us.

If we don't care about fish, who will? Who are the advocates for fish, if not fishermen? There are millions of us, and we could have formidable political clout. We need to be organized in order to use it, though.

In a related vein, who's going to take the torch for these types of battles in the future? Your kids are. The kids down the street. The kids across town, who you don't even know. You need (yes, <u>you</u>, dear reader) to take kids fishing, every chance you get.

I was once a school teacher. I can assure you that there are a lot of kids out there who would love to go fishing but never get a chance. You may know some- your kids, your nieces or nephews, your grandchildren, or neighborhood kids. If you belong to a fishing club you could organize a fishing day for kids, something I do every year with the help of the Backcountry Flyfishing Association, the Indian River Guides Association, the Kiwanis Club of East Orlando, and the Boys and Girls Clubs of Central Florida.

Share your knowledge with a local scout pack. They need to know, there's a fishing merit badge. You'll be doing them a service, and you'll feel better for doing it.

So please, take a kid fishing. A future with clean water and plenty of fish depends on it.

And, as a practical matter, when you get too old and feeble to go fishing by yourself anymore, hopefully those kids you took out so many years back will now take you!

Finally, please remember to use courtesy and etiquette while out on the water. Treat others the way you'd like to be treated. And good luck to you as you're fishing for redfish in the Indian River Lagoon.

The author with two girls who were members of the Boys and Girls Clubs of Central Florida when we had our annual Kids Fishing Day on the Indian River Lagoon. One of them had never been fishing before, and this fish was a thrilling event in her life. Share the love– take a kid fishing!

Index

The Resource Catalog: -INFORMATION-
from Argonaut Publishing Company.

Visit Our On-Line Store at www.spottedtail.com!

Books

Flyrodding Florida Salt– How and Where to Catch Fish on Flies in the Sunshine State
By Capt. John A. Kumiski

Do you like fumbling around when fishing new areas, trying to fit all the pieces together so that you can find a few fish?

This book contains all the information you need to fly fish successfully almost anywhere on Florida's lengthy coastline. Featuring interviews with Florida's top fly anglers, the book solves the problem of "how-to" by explaining what tackle to use, which techniques to try, and what you can expect to catch.

It solves the "where-to" problem with interviews of Florida's premier fly fishing guides. In these interviews they reveal their favorite spots and how to fish them, including many of their most closely guarded secrets.

It solves the "with what" problem by telling you what flies you need in order to have success, and how to tie them or where to buy them.

"The best part of Flyrodding Florida Salt is the extensive where to go section that blankets the coast by area with not only tips on specific fishing spots, but areas for wading, hand powered boats, boat fishing, best flies and techniques, access, local fly shops, boat rentals, guides, and other attractions and accommodations. For any saltwater fly rodder living in Florida or going there sometime, this book is a must read." **-C. Boyd Pfeiffer**

Before you visit the Sunshine State, get this book!

Flyrodding Florida Salt, 240 pp., paperback,......................$29.95

Visit Our On-Line Store at www.spottedtail.com!

Fishing the Space Coast- An Angler's Guide (Ponce de Leon Inlet to Sebastian Inlet)
by Capt. John A. Kumiski

Do You Want to Catch Fish on Florida's Space Coast?
This stretch of the Florida's Atlantic Coast and the adjacent Indian River Lagoon system offers world class angling for redfish, black drum, spotted seatrout, tripletail, and more. In addition, snook, tarpon, cobia, Spanish and king mackerel, little tunny, jack crevalle, bluefish, barracuda, sharks, and many other species can be found in these waters at various times of the year. Do you know how to catch them?
This book will make you a better fisherman. You will learn:
*How-to choose rods, reels, lines, lures, baits, rigging, and techniques that work here.
*When to fish. The fishery changes with the seasons. This book will help you adjust your strategies.
*Where to fish. Aerial photographs pinpoint hot spots all along the Space Coast.

Many of the Space Coast's finest fishing guides shared secrets contained in this book, such well known anglers as Eric Davis, Kent Gibbens, Fred Hill, Mike Hakala, Terry Parsons, Rodney Smith, and many more.

Fishing the Space Coast, 120 pages, paperback, $19.95

How and Where to Catch Redfish in the Indian River Lagoon System
By Capt. John Kumiski

Twenty plus years of hard won information, based on the author's own experiences, are stuffed into this little gem's 96 pages. Whether you're fishing from shore, wading, using a hand powered boat or a motor skiff, pick the right tackle, baits, and lures, then use it all correctly in all the right spots. Aerial photos pinpoint locations where redfish are usually found.

How and Where to Catch Redfish in the Indian River Lagoon System, 96 pages, paperback, $9.95

Sport Fish of Florida   by Vic Dunaway

Vic's long needed book identifies 231 species of Florida fishes, everything from billfish to baitfish. All are illustrated in full color and include scientific and common names, distinguishing features, food value, average and record sizes, range throughout Florida, habitats, game qualities, and best fishing methods.

Visit Our On-Line Store at www.spottedtail.com!

Sport Fish of Florida, 256 pp., paperback, $16.95

Vic Dunaway's Complete Book of Bait, Rigs, and Tackle
by Vic Dunaway

This book covers everything that might be implied by the title-spin, plug, and fly tackle, hooks, sinkers, floats, lines, leaders, knots, fishing accessories, and rigging methods for both natural and artificial baits.

Vic Dunaway's Complete Book of Bait, Rigs, and Tackle, 224 pp., paperback, $16.95

The Florida Atlas and Gazetteer   from DeLorme Mapping

Are you tired of getting lost trying to find those out-of-the way fishing spots? The Florida Atlas and Gazetteer solves your problem! Containing detailed road maps of the entire state, this book is an invaluable resource when finding your way from point A to point B on Florida's highway system is your highest priority.

The Florida Atlas and Gazetteer, 128 pp., paperback. $19.95

-Fishing Maps-

Pasadena Top Spot Fishing Maps pride themselves on making reliable, accurate, waterproof charts with well marked fishing areas. Important information such as the best times of year, types of fish available, artificial fish habitats, and underwater structure are all shown in an easy to read format.

-Homosassa area, N-201
-Tampa Bay area, N-202
-Charlotte Harbor area, N-203
-Ten Thousand Islands area, N-204
-Everglades Park area, N-206
-Florida Bay area, N-207
-Middle Keys area, N-208
-Lower Keys area, N-209
-Miami area, N-211
-Fort Lauderdale area, N-212
-Palm Beach area, N-213
-Jupiter to Stuart area, N-214
-Stuart to South Fort Pierce and St. Lucie area, N-215

Visit Our On-Line Store at www.spottedtail.com!

Fishing Maps, con't.
-Fort Pierce to Vero Beach area, N-216
-Sebastian Inlet and Palm Bay area, N-217
-Cape Canaveral area, N-218
-Mosquito Lagoon area, N-219
-Daytona Beach to Jacksonville area, N-221
-Port St. Joe to Apalachicola; Carabelle to Lighthouse Point, N-230
-Panacea to Apalachee Bay; Steinhatchee to Cedar Key North, N-231

Top Spot Maps, $15.95 each

-Special Reports-

Special Reports by Capt. John Kumiski provide the detailed how-to and where-to information you need to step into a new area or situation and fish confidently and successfully. The five page reports are updated constantly.

The Keys
-How to Find and Catch Bonefish on Long Key,   SR-LK
-How to Find and Catch Bonefish at Pennekamp State Park,   SR-KL
-Fishing Keys Bridges, SR-KB
-Fishing the Keys from a Houseboat, SR-KH
The Everglades
-How to Find and Catch Fish at Flamingo, Everglades National Park, SR-FF
-Day Trips for Canoeing Anglers from Flamingo, Everglades National Park, SR-CF
-How to Find and Catch Backcountry Snook from Flamingo, Everglades National Park,   SR-FS
-Fishing The Cape Sable Area, Everglades National Park, SR-CS
-Fishing Chatham Bend, Everglades National Park, SR-CB
-Fishing Lostman's River, Everglades National Park, SR-LR
-Fishing and Canoe Camping the Everglades, SR-EC
-Fishing for Cape Sable Seatrout, SR-ES
-Fishing the Everglades from a Houseboat, SR-EH
-How to Find and Catch Fish in the10,000 Islands, Everglades National Park, SR-TI
-Everglades Tarpon, SR-ET
Jacksonville and Vicinity
-How to Find and Catch Redfish in Nassau Sound, SR-NS
-Fishing for Redfish in Jacksonville's Backcountry, SR-JR
-Fishing Opportunities in Cumberland Sound, SR-OC

Visit Our On-Line Store at www.spottedtail.com!

Special Reports, con't.
East Central Florida
-How to Find and Catch Redfish at the Merritt Island National Wildlife Refuge, SR-MI
-Fishing at Ponce Inlet and New Smyrna Beach, Canaveral National Seashore, SR-CN
-Fishing the Banana River Manatee Refuge, SR-MR
-Tactics for Sebastian River Tarpon, SR-SR
-Orlando as a Fishing Destination, SR-OF
-Fly Fishing for Bass and Bream in the Wekiva River, SR-WR
-How to Catch Summer Seatrout in the Mosquito Lagoon, SR-SS
-Floating Florida's Spring Creeks for Bass and Bream, SR-SC
-Fishing the Intracoastal Waterway at Daytona/New Smyrna, SR-DB
-Fishing Opportunities Along Cape Canaveral Beaches, SR-CC
-Fishing Opportunities Along the Jupiter Coast, SR-JF
Southwest Florida
-How to Find and Catch Fish in Bull Bay, Charlotte Harbor, SR-CH
-Fishing Captiva Pass and Redfish Pass, SR-CP
-How to Find and Catch Pine Island Redfish, SR-PI
-Fishing at Cayo Costa State Park, SR-CY
-Southwest Florida's Beach Tarpon Run, SR-BT
-Charlotte Harbor's Winter Snook, SR-WS

West Central Florida
-Fly Fishing for Homosassa Tarpon, SR-HT
-Fishing Opportunities at Cedar Key, SR-CK

Saltwater Fly Fishing
-How to Choose your Fishing Guide, SR-CG
-Constructing Saltwater Fly Rod Leader Systems, SR-LS
-Practical Fly Selection for Florida's Saltwater, SR-SF
-Getting Started in Saltwater Fly Fishing, SR-GS
-A Primer for Waders, SR-PW
-How to Increase Your Ability to See Fish, SR-HS
-How to Fight Big Fish Successfully with Light Tackle, SR-BF
-Fly Fishing for Jack Crevalle, SR-JC
-Getting Started in Tying Flies for Saltwater, SR-FT
-Tying and Using Crab Patterns, SR-UC
-A Guide to Fly Fishing from Canoes, SR-FC
Miscellaneous
-Improve Your Fishing Photography, SR-FP
-Practical Tips for Redfish on the Surface, SR-RT

Special Reports, $6.95 each, or three for $17.95

Visit Our On-Line Store at www.spottedtail.com!

Videos and DVD's

Here at Argonaut Publishing Company we have to admit that we prefer books. However, some videos are of such extremely high quality, and can illustrate some topics so much better than can the written word, that we feel compelled to offer the following, with our highest recommendations.

The Art of Fly Casting with Chico Fernandez
Filmed in a specially constructed studio, this film shows the difference between a good cast and a bad cast and shows how best to execute the former. Chico has been fly casting for over 40 years, and this is the finest, most comprehensive video available on how to fly cast.

The Art of Fly Casting with Chico Fernandez, VHS, 37 minutes, $29.95

Borski Ties Flies, Volume 1, featuring Tim Borski
In the studio innovative tier and artist Tim Borski shows how to tie five of his flies (the Green Zima, Haystack, laid up tarpon fly, Big Orange Shark Fly, and Chernobyl Crab) in an easy, step by step format. Then he goes out on the water to show how to fish them. The on-the-water footage, all shot on location in the Florida Keys, is simply spectacular.

Borski Ties Flies, Vol. 1, DVD, 62 minutes, $24.95

Shipping Information

If your order is between:	Standard shipping cost is:	Priority shipping cost is:
$1.00 to 30.00	$4.95	$6.95
$30.01 to 65.00	$7.95	$9.95
$65.01 to 100.00	$10.95	$14.95
Over $100.00	No charge	$25.00

See the order form on the last page!

Order Form

You can contact us by mail, email, telephone, fax (call first!), or <u>order from our online catalog</u>, **www.spottedtail.com**. If sending a check, please make payable to:

Argonaut Publishing Company
284 Clearview Road
Chuluota, FL 32766

-407.977.5207 (phone and fax)
-email: spottedtail@spottedtail.com
-Website: www.spottedtail.com

If there is no one in the office when you call, please leave a message. Please- speak slowly!
1) Tell us who you are and where you want the order shipped.
2) Tell us what you would like to order.
3) Tell how you would like to pay (if by credit card, please leave the number and expiration date).
4) Florida residents, be prepared to pay 7 percent sales tax.
5) Shipping costs depend on what you order and how you want it shipped (see chart on previous page.) Standard shipping is free on orders over $100.00. On in-stock items, orders usually ship the same day or the next day.

Or use the handy order form on the following page!

Thank you for your business!

Ship to:_____

Street_____

City_____

State_____ Zip_____

Phone_____

Quantity	Description (title and author)	Price	Total

Method of Payment: Credit Card Check Money Order	Merchandise Total	
	FL Delivery, add 7% sales tax	
Credit Card #_____	Shipping and Handling (see p. 239)	
_____ Expiration Date _____	**Amount Enclosed**	
Signature _____		